Wonderful ways to prepare

VEGETARIAN DISHES

by JO ANN SHIRLEY

Wonderful ways to prepare

VEGETARIAN DISHES

PLAYMORE INC. NEW YORK USA
UNDER ARRANGEMENT WITH
WALDMAN PUBLISHING CORP.

AYERS & JAMES
SYDNEY AUSTRALIA

STAFFORD PEMBERTON PUBLISHING
KNUTSFORD UNITED KINGDOM

FIRST PUBLISHED 1979

PUBLISHED IN THE USA
BY PLAYMORE INC.
UNDER ARRANGEMENT WITH
WALDMAN PUBLISHING CORP

PUBLISHED IN AUSTRALIA
BY AYERS & JAMES
CROWS NEST. AUSTRALIA

PUBLISHED IN AUSTRALIA
BY AYERS & JAMES
CROWS NEST. AUSTRALIA

PUBLISHED IN THE UNITED KINGDOM
BY STAFFORD PEMBERTON PUBLISHING
KNUTSFORD CHESHIRE

ISBN 0 86908 158 6

OVEN TEMPERATURE GUIDE

Description	Gas		Electric		Mark
	C	F	C	F	
Cool	100	200	110	225	¼
Very Slow	120	250	120	250	½
Slow	150	300	150	300	1-2
Moderately slow	160	325	170	340	3
Moderate	180	350	200	400	4
Moderately hot	190	375	220	425	5-6
Hot	200	400	230	450	6-7
Very hot	230	450	250	475	8-9

LIQUID MEASURES

IMPERIAL	METRIC
1 teaspoon	5 ml
1 tablespoon	20 ml
2 fluid ounces (½ cup)	62.5 ml
4 fluid ounces (½ cup)	125 ml
8 fluid ounces (1 cup)	250 ml
1 pint (16 ounces — 2 cups)*	500 ml

* (The imperial pint is equal to 20 fluid ounces.)

SOLID MEASURES

AVOIRDUPOIS	METRIC
1 ounce	30 g
4 ounces (¼ lb)	125 g
8 ounces (½ lb)	250 g
12 ounces (¾ lb)	375 g
16 ounces (1 lb)	500 g
24 ounces (1½ lb)	750 g
32 ounces (2 lb)	1000 g (1 kg)

CUP AND SPOON REPLACEMENTS FOR OUNCES

INGREDIENT	½ oz	1 oz	2 oz	3 oz	4 oz	5 oz	6 oz	7 oz	8 oz
Almonds, ground	2 T	¼ C	½ C	¾ C	1¼ C	1⅓ C	1⅔ C	2 C	2¼ C
slivered	6 t	¼ C	½ C	¾ C	1 C	1⅓ C	1⅔ C	2 C	2¼ C
whole	2 T	¼ C	⅓ C	½ C	¾ C	1 C	1¼ C	1⅓ C	1½ C
Apples, dried whole	3 T	½ C	1 C	1⅓ C	2 C	2⅓ C	2¾ C	3⅓ C	3¾ C
Apricots, chopped	2 T	¼ C	½ C	¾ C	1 C	1¼ C	1½ C	1¾ C	2 C
whole	2 T	3 T	½ C	⅔ C	1 C	1¼ C	1⅓ C	1½ C	1¾ C
Arrowroot	1 T	2 T	⅓ C	½ C	⅔ C	¾ C	1 C	1¼ C	1⅓ C
Baking Powder	1 T	2 T	⅓ C	½ C	⅔ C	¾ C	1 C	1 C	1¼ C
Baking Soda	1 T	2 T	⅓ C	½ C	⅔ C	¾ C	1 C	1 C	1¼ C
Barley	1 T	2 T	¼ C	½ C	⅔ C	¾ C	1 C	1 C	1¼ C
Breadcrumbs, dry	2 T	¼ C	½ C	¾ C	1 C	1¼ C	1½ C	1¾ C	2 C
soft	¼ C	½ C	1 C	1½ C	2 C	2½ C	3 C	3⅔ C	4¼ C
Biscuit Crumbs	2 T	¼ C	½ C	¾ C	1¼ C	1⅓ C	1⅔ C	2 C	2¼ C
Butter	3 t	6 t	¼ C	⅓ C	½ C	⅔ C	¾ C	1 C	1 C
Cheese, grated, lightly packed,									
natural cheddar	6 t	¼ C	½ C	¾ C	1 C	1¼ C	1½ C	1¾ C	2 C
Processed cheddar	5 t	2 T	⅓ C	⅔ C	¾ C	1 C	1¼ C	1½ C	1⅔ C
Parmesan, Romano	6 t	¼ C	½ C	¾ C	1 C	1⅓ C	1⅔ C	2 C	2¼ C
Cherries, candied, chopped	1 T	2 T	⅓ C	½ C	¾ C	1 C	1 C	1⅓ C	1½ C
whole	1 T	2 T	⅓ C	½ C	⅔ C	¾ C	1 C	1¼ C	1⅓ C
Cocoa	2 T	¼ C	½ C	¾ C	1¼ C	1⅓ C	1⅔ C	2 C	2¼ C
Coconut, desiccated	2 T	⅓ C	⅔ C	1 C	1⅓ C	1⅔ C	2 C	2⅓ C	2⅔ C
shredded	⅓ C	⅔ C	1¼ C	1¾ C	2½ C	3 C	3⅔ C	4⅓ C	5 C
Cornstarch	6 t	3 T	½ C	⅔ C	1 C	1¼ C	1½ C	1⅔ C	2 C
Corn Syrup	2 t	1 T	2 T	¼ C	⅓ C	½ C	½ C	⅔ C	⅔ C
Coffee, ground	2 T	⅓ C	⅔ C	1 C	1⅓ C	1⅔ C	2 C	2⅓ C	2⅔ C
instant	3 T	½ C	1 C	1⅓ C	1¾ C	2¼ C	2⅔ C	3 C	3½ C
Cornflakes	½ C	1 C	2 C	3 C	4¼ C	5¼ C	6¼ C	7⅓ C	8⅓ C
Cream of Tartar	1 T	2 T	⅓ C	½ C	⅔ C	¾ C	1 C	1 C	1¼ C
Currants	1 T	2 T	⅓ C	⅔ C	¾ C	1 C	1¼ C	1½ C	1⅔ C
Custard Powder	6 t	3 T	½ C	⅔ C	1 C	1¼ C	1½ C	1⅔ C	2 C
Dates, chopped	1 T	2 T	⅓ C	⅔ C	¾ C	1 C	1¼ C	1½ C	1⅔ C
whole, pitted	1 T	2 T	⅓ C	½ C	¾ C	1 C	1¼ C	1⅓ C	1½ C
Figs, chopped	1 T	2 T	⅓ C	½ C	¾ C	1 C	1 C	1⅓ C	1½ C
Flour, all-purpose or cake	6 t	¼ C	½ C	¾ C	1 C	1¼ C	1½ C	1¾ C	2 C
wholemeal	6 t	3 T	½ C	⅔ C	1 C	1¼ C	1⅓ C	1⅔ C	1¾ C
Fruit, mixed	1 T	2 T	⅓ C	½ C	¾ C	1 C	1¼ C	1⅓ C	1½ C
Gelatin	5 t	2 T	⅓ C	½ C	¾ C	1 C	1 C	1¼ C	1½ C
Ginger, crystallised pieces	1 T	2 T	⅓ C	½ C	¾ C	1 C	1¼ C	1⅓ C	1½ C
ground	6 t	⅓ C	½ C	¾ C	1¼ C	1½ C	1¾ C	2 C	2¼ C
preserved, heavy syrup	1 T	2 T	⅓ C	½ C	⅔ C	¾ C	1 C	1 C	1¼ C
Glucose, liquid	2 t	1 T	2 T	¼ C	⅓ C	½ C	½ C	⅔ C	⅔ C
Haricot Beans	1 T	2 T	⅓ C	½ C	⅔ C	¾ C	1 C	1 C	1¼ C

In this table, t represents teaspoonful, T represents tablespoonful and C represents cupful.

CUP AND SPOON REPLACEMENTS FOR OUNCES (Cont.)

INGREDIENT	½ oz	1 oz	2 oz	3 oz	4 oz	5 oz	6 oz	7 oz	8 oz
Honey	2 t	1 T	2 T	¼ C	⅓ C	½ C	½ C	⅔ C	⅔ C
Jam	2 t	1 T	2 T	¼ C	⅓ C	½ C	½ C	⅔ C	¾ C
Lentils	1 T	2 T	⅓ C	½ C	⅔ C	¾ C	1 C	1 C	1¼ C
Macaroni (see pasta)									
Milk Powder, full cream	2 T	¼ C	½ C	¾ C	1¼ C	1⅓ C	1⅔ C	2 C	2¼ C
non fat	2 T	⅓ C	¾ C	1¼ C	1½ C	2 C	2⅓ C	2¾ C	3¼ C
Nutmeg	6 t	3 T	½ C	⅔ C	¾ C	1 C	1¼ C	1½ C	1⅔ C
Nuts, chopped	6 t	¼ C	½ C	¾ C	1 C	1¼ C	1½ C	1¾ C	2 C
Oatmeal	1 T	2 T	½ C	⅔ C	¾ C	1 C	1¼ C	1½ C	1⅔ C
Olives, whole	1 T	2 T	⅓ C	⅔ C	¾ C	1 C	1¼ C	1½ C	1⅔ C
sliced	1 T	2 T	⅓ C	⅔ C	¾ C	1 C	1¼ C	1½ C	1⅔ C
Pasta, short (e.g. macaroni)	1 T	2 T	⅓ C	⅔ C	¾ C	1 C	1¼ C	1½ C	1⅔ C
Peaches, dried & whole	1 T	2 T	⅓ C	⅔ C	¾ C	1 C	1¼ C	1½ C	1⅔ C
chopped	6 t	¼ C	½ C	¾ C	1 C	1¼ C	1½ C	1¾ C	2 C
Peanuts, shelled, raw, whole	1 T	2 T	⅓ C	½ C	¾ C	1 C	1¼ C	1⅓ C	1½ C
roasted	1 T	2 T	⅓ C	⅔ C	¾ C	1 C	1¼ C	1½ C	1⅔ C
Peanut Butter	3 t	6 t	3 T	⅓ C	½ C	½ C	⅔ C	¾ C	1 C
Peas, split	1 T	2 T	⅓ C	½ C	⅔ C	¾ C	1 C	1 C	1¼ C
Peel, mixed	1 T	2 T	⅓ C	½ C	¾ C	1 C	1 C	1¼ C	1½ C
Potato, powder	1 T	2 T	¼ C	⅓ C	½ C	⅔ C	¾ C	1 C	1¼ C
flakes	¼ C	½ C	1 C	1⅓ C	2 C	2⅓ C	2¾ C	3⅓ C	3¾ C
Prunes, chopped	1 T	2 T	⅓ C	½ C	⅔ C	¾ C	1 C	1¼ C	1⅓ C
whole pitted	1 T	2 T	⅓ C	½ C	⅔ C	¾ C	1 C	1 C	1¼ C
Raisins	2 T	¼ C	⅓ C	½ C	¾ C	1 C	1 C	1⅓ C	1½ C
Rice, short grain, raw	1 T	2 T	¼ C	½ C	⅔ C	¾ C	1 C	1 C	1¼ C
long grain, raw	1 T	2 T	⅓ C	½ C	¾ C	1 C	1¼ C	1⅓ C	1½ C
Rice Bubbles	⅔ C	1¼ C	2½ C	3⅔ C	5 C	6¼ C	7½ C	8¾ C	10 C
Rolled Oats	2 T	⅓ C	⅔ C	1 C	1⅓ C	1¾ C	2 C	2½ C	2¾ C
Sago	2 T	¼ C	⅓ C	½ C	¾ C	1 C	1 C	1¼ C	1½ C
Salt, common	3 t	6 t	¼ C	⅓ C	½ C	⅔ C	¾ C	1 C	1 C
Semolina	1 T	2 T	⅓ C	½ C	¾ C	1 C	1 C	1⅓ C	1½ C
Spices	6 t	3 T	¼ C	⅓ C	½ C	½ C	⅔ C	¾ C	1 C
Sugar, plain	3 t	6 t	¼ C	⅓ C	½ C	⅔ C	¾ C	1 C	1 C
confectioners'	1 T	2 T	⅓ C	½ C	¾ C	1 C	1 C	1¼ C	1½ C
moist brown	1 T	2 T	⅓ C	½ C	¾ C	1 C	1 C	1⅓ C	1½ C
Tapioca	1 T	2 T	⅓ C	½ C	⅔ C	¾ C	1 C	1¼ C	1⅓ C
Treacle	2 t	1 T	2 T	¼ C	⅓ C	½ C	½ C	⅔ C	⅔ C
Walnuts, chopped	2 T	¼ C	½ C	¾ C	1 C	1¼ C	1½ C	1¾ C	2 C
halved	2 T	⅓ C	⅔ C	1 C	1¼ C	1½ C	1¾ C	2¼ C	2½ C
Yeast, dried	6 t	3 T	½ C	⅔ C	1 C	1¼ C	1⅓ C	1⅔ C	1¾ C
compressed	3 t	6 t	3 T	⅓ C	½ C	½ C	⅔ C	¾ C	1 C

In this table, t represents teaspoonful, T represents tablespoonful and C represents cupful.

Contents

Vegetarian Recipes

Haricot Bean and Macaroni Soup

½ cup dried haricot beans
10 cups (2½ liters) water
2 medium onions, chopped
3 cloves garlic, minced
3 stalks celery, chopped

4 tablespoons oil
salt and thyme
1 cup short macaroni
chopped parsley
Parmesan cheese

1. Soak the beans in enough water to cover overnight.
2. Put the beans in a large saucepan with the water and slowly bring to a boil. Simmer until the beans are tender.
3. Saute the onion, garlic and celery in the oil until they are golden brown.
4. Add the vegetables to the beans and bring to a boil again. Skim off any froth that rises to the top.
5. Add salt and thyme to taste and simmer for 15 minutes.
6. Add the macaroni and cook until the macaroni is tender.
7. Serve sprinkled with chopped parsley and Parmesan cheese.

Serves 6-8.

Cabbage Soup

½ cabbage, shredded
3 medium potatoes, cubed
8 cups (2 liters) onion stock
salt and pepper
grated cheese

1. Simmer the cabbage and potatoes in the stock for 30 minutes.
2. Season to taste with salt and pepper.
3. Serve topped with grated cheese.

Serves 4-6.

Spanish Vegetable Soup

2 medium onions, chopped
4 tablespoons oil
½ lb (250 g) zucchini, sliced
2 large potatoes, cubed
2 cloves garlic, sliced in slivers
2 teaspoons paprika

1 lb (500 g) tomatoes, peeled and chopped
6 cups (1½ liters) onion stock
1 teaspoon basil
salt

1. Saute the onions in the oil until transparent.
2. Add the zucchini, potatoes, garlic and paprika and cook over a low heat for ten minutes.
3. Add the tomatoes and simmer for ten minutes.
4. Stir in the stock and basil and simmer, covered, for ½ hour.
5. Season to taste with salt and simmer uncovered for five minutes.

Serves 4-6.

Cream of Tomato Soup

3 lb (1½ kg) ripe tomatoes
2 small onions, chopped
¼ cup (65 g) butter
3 teaspoons chopped fresh dill

2½ cups (625 ml) cream
1 teaspoon brown sugar
1 teaspoon salt
freshly ground black pepper

1. Blanch the tomatoes and peel. Chop them into small bits.
2. Saute the onions in the butter for three minutes.
3. Add the tomatoes and the dill and simmer for 30 minutes. Press through a strainer and return to the saucepan. Heat throughly. Remove from heat.
4. Heat the cream with the sugar, then slowly pour into the soup, stirring constantly.
5. Add the salt and pepper and serve immediately.

(A couple of tablespoons of brandy added just before serving is delicious.)

Serves 6.

Fresh Pea Soup with Dumplings

4 cups shelled peas
5 cups (1¼ liters) water
1 teaspoon sugar
1 cup (250 ml) white wine
salt and pepper
⅓ cup (85 g) butter
5½ tablespoons plain flour

Dumplings:
½ cup (125 g) butter
2 eggs
½ cup flour
¼ teaspoon cinnamon
salt

1. Cook the peas in the water with the sugar for about 20 minutes or until tender. Drain.
2. Press the peas through a strainer or puree in an electric blender. Return to a large saucepan.
3. Add the wine and salt and pepper to taste.
4. Melt the butter in a small saucepan. Stir in the flour and cook for one minute.
5. Add a little of the pea soup and to the flour butter. Mix well, then slowly add this mixture to the soup, stirring constantly.
6. To make the dumplings, first soften the butter.
7. Lightly beat the eggs and mix them with the flour.
8. Add to the softened butter with the cinnamon and salt to taste.
9. Drop the dumplings a teaspoon at a time into the boiling soup. After they have risen to the top, cook for another five minutes.

Serves 6.

Cream of Spinach Soup

1½ lb (750 g) spinach
1 large onion, chopped
4 tablespoons (60 g) butter
5½ tablespoons plain flour

water
2½ cups (625 ml) milk
salt
½ teaspoon nutmeg

1. Wash the spinach thoroughly several times. Put in a saucepan with no extra water added, cover and cook for seven minutes. Drain but reserve the liquid.
2. Saute the onion in the butter until golden brown in a large saucepan.
3. Stir in the flour and cook, stirring constantly, for three minutes.
4. Add enough water to the liquid from the spinach to make up 2½ cups (625 ml). Stir into the onion mixture.
5. Slowly add the milk, stirring constantly.
6. Chop the spinach and add to the soup with salt to taste and the nutmeg. Heat thoroughly.

Serves 4.

Cream of Cauliflower Soup

1 cauliflower
4 cups (1 liter) milk
1½ cups (375 ml) vegetable
   stock or water

4 tablespoons (60 g) butter
4 tablespoons plain flour
salt and pepper
chopped parsley

1. Cut the cauliflower into flowerets and rinse in cold water.
2. Combine the milk and stock or water and bring to a boil.
3. Add the cauliflower and cook until tender.
4. Press the cauliflower with the liquid through a strainer or puree in an electric blender.
5. In a large saucepan, melt the butter and stir in the flour. Cook for two minutes over a low heat.
6. Slowly pour into the cauliflower mixture, stirring constantly, until smooth.
7. Add the salt and pepper to taste and cook for ten minutes.
8. Serve sprinkled with chopped parsley.

Serves 4-6.

Cheese Soup

⅓ cup (85 g) butter
4 tablespoons plain flour
1½ cups (375 ml) milk
3 cups (750 ml) water
4 tablespoons cream

salt
¼ teaspoon nutmeg
1 cup grated Gruyere cheese
chopped parsley

1. Melt the butter in a large saucepan. Stir in the flour and cook over a low heat for one minute.
2. Slowly add the milk, stirring constantly, until smooth.
3. Add the water and blend thoroughly. Cook over a low heat for 20 minutes.
4. Stir in the cream, salt to taste and the nutmeg. Cook for three minutes. Remove from heat.
5. Add the cheese and stir until melted.
6. Serve sprinkled with chopped parsley.

Serves 4.

Chilled Lemon Soup

6 cups (1½ liters) water
1 cup sugar
1 cup (250 ml) lemon juice
⅓ cup (85 ml) orange juice
2½ tablespoons grated lemon rind

4 tablespoons grated orange rind
2½ tablespoons cornstarch
2 egg whites
4 teaspoons sugar

1. Mix the water with the sugar in a large saucepan and bring to a boil. Reduce heat and simmer for ten minutes.
2. Add the lemon and orange juice and rinds and cook for five minutes.
3. Mix the cornstarch with water to make a thin paste. Slowly add to the soup, stirring constantly. Cook for another ten minutes. Cool.
4. Beat the egg whites with the sugar until stiff.
5. Serve the soup with a spoonful of egg white fluff on the top.

Serves 4-6.

Chilled Cherry Soup

1½ lb (750 g) dark cherries	4 tablespoons lemon juice
6 cups (1½ liters) water	2½ tablespoons cornstarch
¼ teaspoon cinnamon	2½ tablespoons cold water
1¼ cups sugar	⅔ cup (165 ml) cream,
grated rind of one lemon	whipped

1. Wash and stone the cherries.
2. Combine the cherries with the water and cinnamon in a large saucepan. Bring to a boil. Reduce heat and simmer for ten minutes.
3. Add the sugar, lemon rind and lemon juice. Cook for five minutes.
4. Mix the cornstarch with the cold water and slowly pour into the soup, stirring constantly. Cook for another ten minutes. Cool.
5. Serve the soup chilled, topped with the whipped cream.

Serves 4-6.

Pureed Vegetable Soup

4 tablespoons (60 g) butter	6 cups (1½ liters) vegetable
½ lb (250 g) carrots, diced	stock or water
1½ lb (750 g) potatoes, peeled	2½ tablespoons cream
and diced	1 teaspoon marjoram
5 stalks celery, sliced	salt and pepper
3 large onions, chopped	
½ lb (250 g) mushrooms, sliced	

1. Melt the butter in a large saucepan and saute the vegetables, stirring occasionally, for ten minutes.
2. Add half the stock and cook until all the vegetables are soft.
3. Press the vegetables and the liquid through a strainer or puree in an electric blender.
4. Return to the saucepan and stir in the rest of the stock or water and bring to a boil.
5. Reduce the heat and stir in the cream, marjoram and salt and pepper to taste. Simmer for 15-20 minutes and serve.

Serves 4-6.

Beet Soup

2 lb (1 kg) beets	2 cloves garlic, minced
1 small cabbage	4 teaspoons (20 g) butter
10 cups (2½ liters) vegetable stock	⅔ cup (165 g) sour cream
3 teaspoons chopped fresh dill	salt and pepper

1. Peel the beets and cut all except two into cubes.
2. Shred three-quarters of the cabbage and add to the stock with the cubed beets, dill and garlic. Bring to a boil. Reduce the heat and simmer for two hours. Strain and return the liquid to the saucepan.
3. Slice the remaining cabbage into strips and grate the beets coarsely.
4. Saute the beets in the butter for two minutes.
5. Add the beets and the sliced cabbage to the liquid and cook for 15 minutes. Remove from the heat.
6. Stir in the sour cream and season to taste with salt and pepper.

Serves 6-8.

Fresh Pea Soup with Eggs

1 medium onion	2½ tablespoons chopped parsley
¼ cup (65 ml) oil	salt and pepper
5 large new potatoes	⅛ teaspoon saffron
6 cups (1½ liters) boiling water	6 eggs
2 lb (1 kg) fresh peas	6 slices French bread
3 cloves garlic, minced	

1. Chop the onion and saute in the oil in a large saucepan until transparent.
2. Peel the potatoes and cut into slices. Add to the onion and stir until coated with the oil.
3. Add the boiling water and cook uncovered for five minutes.
4. Shell the peas and add to the soup with the garlic, parsley, salt and pepper to taste, and saffron. Mix well, cover and cook gently until the potatoes are cooked and the peas are tender.
5. Carefully break the eggs, one at a time, into the soup so they poach in the simmering liquid for about four minutes.
6. Put a slice of French bread in each soup bowl and carefully put an egg on top. Spoon the soup into the bowls.

Serves 6.

Corn Chowder with Cheese

2 medium potatoes, diced
2 cups (500 ml) boiling salted water
1 bay leaf
½ teaspoon cumin seeds
¼ cup (65 g) butter
2 medium onions, minced
4 tablespoons plain flour
1½ cups (375 ml) cream

1 can (310 g) corn kernels or 1½ cups fresh corn kernels
1½ tablespoons chopped chives
1½ tablespoons chopped parsley
salt and pepper
1 cup grated cheese
⅓ cup (85 ml) white wine

1. Cook the potatoes in the boiling salted water with the bay leaf and cumin seeds until tender. Do not drain.
2. Melt the butter in a saucepan and saute the onions until transparent.
3. Add the flour to the onions and mix well.
4. Slowly pour on the cream, stirring constantly.
5. Add the onion mixture to the potatoes with the corn kernels, chives, parsley and salt and pepper to taste. Simmer for about ten minutes.
6. Add the cheese and wine and mix well. Cook over a very low heat, stirring constantly, until the cheese is melted.

Serves 4-6.

Sorrel Soup

1 medium onion, chopped
3 tablespoons (45 g) butter
1 lb (500 g) sorrel
1 small lettuce

4 cups (1 liter) stock
2 eggs yolks
1 cup freshly made croutons

1. Saute the onion in the butter in a large saucepan for five minutes.
2. Thoroughly wash the sorrel and the lettuce. Drain and coarsely chop them.
3. Add to the onion, stir well and cook until they are limp.
4. Pour on the boiling stock. Season to taste with salt and pepper. Bring to a boil. Reduce heat and simmer, uncovered, for ten minutes.
5. Put the soup through a strainer.
6. Return it to the saucepan and bring to a boil.
7. Beat the egg yolks. Add a little of the soup to them and mix well. Pour the mixture back into the soup, stirring constantly. Cook over a very low heat until thickened.
8. Serve with a knob of butter on each serving and the croutons.

Serves 4-6.

Zucchini with Eggs

1 lb (500 g) zucchini
3 tablespoons (45 g) butter
½ cup fresh bread crumbs
¼ cup Parmesan cheese
1 medium onion, chopped

2 teaspoons butter
salt and pepper
6 eggs, beaten
2½ tablespoons oil
extra Parmesan cheese

1. Slice the zucchini and saute in the butter for ten minutes over a low heat.
2. In a large bowl mix together the zucchini, bread crumbs and Parmesan cheese.
3. Saute the onion in the two teaspoons of butter for five minutes.
4. Add the onion to the zucchini mixture with the beaten eggs.
5. Heat the oil in a large fry pan and pour the zucchini and egg mixture into it. Cover and cook until the bottom is set and slightly brown.
6. Sprinkle with more Parmesan cheese and put under a hot broiler. Cook until set and golden brown.
7. Cut into wedges and serve.

(This dish may be eaten hot or cold. If you are going to eat it cold, substitute oil for the butter.)

Serves 6.

Greek Salad

½ lb (250 g) fetta cheese
1 lettuce
4 large tomatoes
¼ lb (125 g) black olives
1 small cucumber

1 large onion
salt and pepper
olive oil
lemon juice

1. Break the fetta cheese into bite-size pieces.
2. Wash and dry the lettuce thoroughly. Break up and put into a bowl with the fetta cheese on top.
3. Quarter the tomatoes and put on the lettuce with the black olives.
4. Peel and slice the cucumber and onion. Lay on top of the tomatoes.
5. Season generously with salt and pepper.
6. Sprinkle with olive oil and set aside until ready to serve.
7. Before serving mix together a dressing of olive oil and lemon juice, pour over the salad and toss gently.

Serves 6.

Cucumber and Yogurt Salad

2 medium cucumbers	4 teaspoons lemon juice
½ medium onion, chopped	⅔ cup (165 g) yogurt
1½ tablespoons chopped chives	salt
1½ tablespoons chopped parsley	paprika

1. Peel the cucumbers and cut into thin slices.
2. Mix together the onion, chives, parsley, lemon juice, yogurt and salt to taste.
3. Pour over the cucumbers and mix thoroughly.
4. Sprinkle with paprika and serve immediately.

Serves 4.

Asparagus Mold

½ lb (250 g) fresh asparagus	1 cup (250 ml) cream, whipped
2½ tablespoons gelatin	salt
3 tablespoons (45 g) butter	pinch of cayenne
2½ tablespoons plain flour	
4 eggs, well beaten	

1. Wash the asparagus very well to remove all the grit. Trim off the tough ends and cook in boiling salted water until tender.
2. Measure one cup (250 ml) of the liquid. Mix the gelatin in ¼ cup. Allow to soak for at least five minutes.
3. Melt the butter and stir in the flour. Cook over a low heat for one minute.
4. Slowly add the remaining asparagus liquid, stirring constantly.
5. Add the eggs, continuing to stir until the mixture is smooth and thick.
6. Add the gelatin and stir until dissolved. Cool.
7. Fold in whipped cream.
8. Cut the tips from the asparagus and line an oiled mold with them.
9. Cut the remaining stalks into one-inch (2½-cm) pieces and stir into the gelatin mixture. Season with salt and pinch of cayenne.
10. Pour into the mold and chill until firm.
11. When set, unmold and serve with French dressing if desired.

Serves 6.

Tomato and Cucumber Salad

1 large cucumber, sliced
4 medium tomatoes, sliced
2 medium onions, sliced
2 teaspoons chopped chives
1½ tablespoons chopped
   parsley

⅓ cup mayonnaise
2½ tablespoons lemon juice
lettuce leaves

1. Gently mix together the cucumber, tomatoes, onions, chives and parsley.
2. Mix together the mayonnaise and lemon juice.
3. Put the cucumbers, tomatoes and onions on the lettuce leaves.
4. Pour the dressing on top and serve.

Serves 4.

Chicory and Orange Salad

¾ lb (375 g) chicory
2 oranges, peeled and sliced
4 teaspoons honey
½ cup (125 g) yogurt
lettuce leaves
chopped parsley

1. Slice the chicory and mix with the orange slices.
2. Blend the honey with the yogurt. Pour over the chicory and oranges and toss until well coated.
3. Serve on crisp lettuce leaves and sprinkle with chopped parsley.

Serves 4.

Beet Mold

2½ tablespoons gelatin	1 teaspoon salt
½ cup (125 ml) cold water	¼ teaspoon black pepper
1 lb (500 g) diced cooked beets	1 cup chopped celery
¼ cup (65 ml) vinegar	1 cup chopped cucumber
¼ cup (65 ml) lemon juice	2 scallions, chopped
⅓ cup sugar	shredded cabbage
	sour cream

1. Soak the gelatin in the cold water for five minutes.
2. Mix together the beets, vinegar, lemon juice, sugar, salt and pepper. Press through a sieve or puree in an electric blender.
3. Pour the beets mixture into a saucepan and heat to boiling.
4. Stir in the gelatin until dissolved. Cool, then chill until partially set.
5. Add the chopped celery, cucumber and scallions. Mix thoroughly.
6. Pour into an oiled mold and chill until set.
7. Unmold onto a bed of shredded cabbage and garnish with sour cream.

Serves 6.

Cauliflower and Carrot Salad

¾ lb (375 g) cauliflower	⅔ cup (165 ml) mayonnaise
4 medium carrots	2½ tablespoons lemon juice
1 medium onion, chopped	salt and pepper
1 teaspoon sugar	lettuce leaves

1. Chop the cauliflower into small pieces.
2. Grate the carrots and mix with the cauliflower and onion.
3. Blend together the sugar, mayonnaise, lemon juice and salt and pepper to taste.
4. Pour over the cauliflower mixture and toss thoroughly.
5. Serve on crisp lettuce leaves.

Serves 4.

Cauliflower a la Greque

1 cauliflower
2 cups (500 ml) water
⅔ cup (165 ml) oil
¼ cup (65 ml) vinegar
½ cup (125 ml) lemon juice
½ teaspoon thyme
½ teaspoon dried mint
1 bay leaf

½ teaspoon coriander
12 peppercorns
1 teaspoon salt
½ cup chopped celery leaves
2 cloves garlic, minced
2½ tablespoons chopped parsley

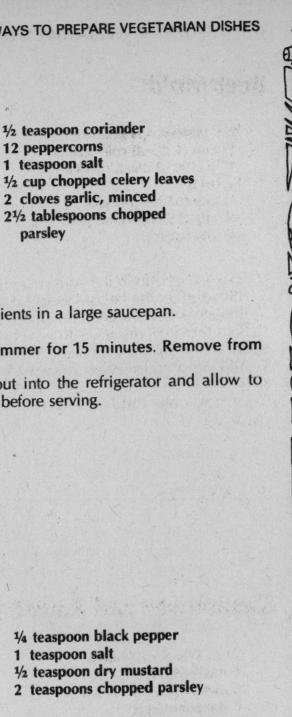

1. Cut the cauliflower into flowerets.
2. Mix together all the remaining ingredients in a large saucepan.
3. Add the cauliflower and mix well.
4. **Bring to a boil. Reduce heat and simmer for 15 minutes. Remove from heat and cool.**
5. When the cauliflower has cooled, put into the refrigerator and allow to marinate for at least 24 hours. Drain before serving.

Serves 6-8.

Leek Salad

10 medium leeks
½ cup (125 ml) oil
¼ cup (65 ml) vinegar
2 cloves garlic, minced

¼ teaspoon black pepper
1 teaspoon salt
½ teaspoon dry mustard
2 teaspoons chopped parsley

1. Cut the roots and the green tops off the leeks. Rinse them under cold water and slice. Boil in salted water for five minutes, then drain and cool in cold water for two minutes.
2. Mix together the oil, vinegar, garlic, black pepper, salt, dry mustard and parsley.
3. Pour the dressing over the leeks and allow to marinate in the refrigerator for two hours.

Serves 6.

Cauliflower and Herb Salad

¾ lb (375 g) cauliflower
¾ cup mayonnaise
4 tablespoons lemon juice
1½ tablespoons chopped
    parsley

2 teaspoons chopped chives
4 teaspoons chopped chervil
2 teaspoons chopped
    marjoram
salt

1. Cut the cauliflower into small pieces.
2. Mix the mayonnaise with the lemon juice, herbs and salt to taste.
3. Pour over the cauliflower and mix thoroughly.

Serves 4.

Beet and Raisin Salad

4 medium beets
1 cup raisins
2 teaspoons brown sugar
¼ cup (65 ml) oil

2 tablespoons lemon juice
lettuce leaves
chopped parsley

1. Peel and grate the beets.
2. Chop the raisins coarsely and mix with the beets and the brown sugar.
3. Mix together the oil and lemon juice.
4. Pour over the beets and raisins and mix well.
5. Serve on crisp lettuce leaves sprinkled with chopped parsley.

Serves 4.

Tomato Salad

1 lb (500 g) tomatoes
1 green pepper
1 red pepper
2½ tablespoons chopped
  chives
¼ cup (65 ml) oil

1 teaspoon cumin seeds
1½ tablespoons vinegar
freshly ground black pepper
salt
2 tablespoons chopped
  parsley

1. Cut the tomatoes into cubes.
2. Remove the seeds from the peppers and slice into thin strips.
3. Mix together the tomatoes, peppers and chives.
4. Heat the oil with the cumin seeds for three minutes. Remove from heat and cool slightly.
5. Add the vinegar and season to taste with pepper and salt.
6. Mix the dressing well, then pour over the vegetables. Toss gently.
7. Cool for about 30 minutes before serving. Sprinkle with chopped parsley just before serving.

Serves 4.

Raw Mushroom Salad

1 lb (500 g) button
  mushrooms
½ cup (125 ml) oil
4 tablespoons vinegar
2½ tablespoons capers
4 tablespoons chopped red
  pepper

¼ teaspoon cayenne
salt and pepper
1 lettuce
2 hard-boiled eggs
2½ tablespoons chopped
  parsley

1. Wipe the mushrooms with a damp cloth and slice them thinly.
2. Mix together the oil, vinegar, capers, red pepper, cayenne and salt and pepper to taste.
3. Add the mushrooms to the dressing and toss lightly. Marinate for about two hours.
4. Wash the lettuce thoroughly and tear into bite-size pieces.
5. Place the lettuce in a salad bowl and spoon the mushrooms with the marinade over the lettuce.
6. Slice or chop the hard-boiled eggs and arrange on top of the mushrooms. Sprinkle with chopped parsley.

Serves 6-8.

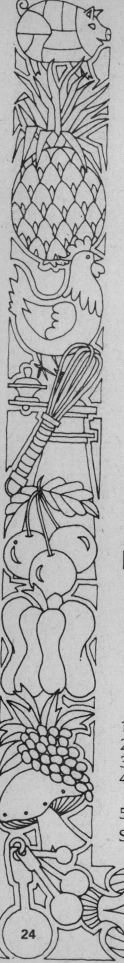

Apple and Carrot Salad

4 medium carrots
4 medium red apples
2½ tablespoons cream
2½ tablespoons lemon juice

1 teaspoon sugar
lettuce leaves
chopped chives

1. Peel the carrots if necessary and grate.
2. Core the apples but do not peel. Grate.
3. Mix together the carrots and apples.
4. Combine the cream with the lemon juice and sugar.
5. Pour over the carrots and apples and mix well.
6. Serve on crisp lettuce leaves and sprinkle with the chopped chives.

Serves 4.

Fig Salad

10 dried figs
4 medium carrots
4 medium red apples
2½ tablespoons ground
   almonds

⅔ cup (165 ml) cream
3 tablespoons lemon juice
lettuce leaves

1. Chop the figs coarsely, peel the carrots if necessary and core the apples.
2. Chop them finely or put them through a mincer.
3. Mix in the ground almonds.
4. Mix together the cream and lemon juice and pour over the fig mixture. Blend thoroughly.
5. Serve on crisp lettuce leaves.

Serves 4.

Date and Apple Salad

16 stoned dates
2 medium red apples
2 medium green apples
2 teaspoons brown sugar

¼ cup (65 ml) cream
4 teaspoons lemon juice
chopped parsley
lettuce leaves

1. Cut the dates into thin slices.
2. Slice and core the apples. Do not peel.
3. Mix the brown sugar with the cream, lemon juice and chopped parsley.
4. Combine the dates, apples and dressing and mix well.
5. Serve on crisp lettuce leaves.

Serves 4.

Apple and Beet Salad

4 medium cooking apples
4 medium raw beets
2 teaspoons brown sugar
⅓ cup (85 ml) oil

2 tablespoons lemon juice
lettuce leaves
finely chopped chives

1. Core the apples but do not peel. Grate finely.
2. Peel the beets and grate finely.
3. Mix the apples and the beets together with the brown sugar.
4. Combine the oil and lemon juice.
5. Pour over the apples and beets and mix well.
6. Serve on crisp lettuce leaves sprinkled with chopped chives.

Serves 4.

Haricot Bean Salad

1 cup dried haricot beans
4 cups (1 liter) water
½ cup (125 ml) oil
2 bay leaves
2 cloves garlic, whole
1 teaspoon salt

Dressing:
½ cup (125 ml) oil
½ cup (125 ml) vinegar

4 tablespoons chopped
  parsley
½ teaspoon oregano
½ teaspoon tarragon
½ teaspoon thyme
½ teaspoon freshly ground
  black pepper
salt
lettuce leaves

1. Rinse the beans and soak them overnight in enough water to cover. Drain.
2. Mix the beans with the water, oil, bay leaves, garlic and salt in a large saucepan. Bring to a boil. Reduce heat and simmer for about two hours or until the beans are tender. Drain and remove the garlic cloves and bay leaves.
3. Beat together all the dressing ingredients except the lettuce.
4. Put the beans in a bowl and pour the dressing over. Mix well, cover and refrigerate for several hours. Serve on top of crisp lettuce leaves.

Serves 6.

Asparagus Meringue

2 lb (1 kg) fresh asparagus
Sauce:
4 tablespoons (60 g) butter
4 tablespoons plain flour
1½ cups (375 ml) hot milk
3 egg yolks, beaten
¼ teaspoon onion salt
1 teaspoon dry mustard
¼ teaspoon cayenne
2½ tablespoons mayonnaise

Meringue:
3 egg whites
¼ teaspoon salt
4 tablespoons mayonnaise
2 teaspoons prepared
mustard
1 teaspoon lemon juice

1. Snap off the tough ends of the asparagus stalks. Cook in boiling salted water until tender. Drain. Place in a well-buttered casserole dish.
2. Melt the butter and stir in the flour. Cook over a low heat for one minute.
3. Slowly add the hot milk, stirring constantly, until thick and smooth.
4. Add a little of the white sauce to the beaten egg yolks. Mix well then beat the egg yolks into the white sauce.
5. Add the onion salt, mustard, cayenne and mayonnaise and mix well. Heat thoroughly.
6. Pour this sauce over the asparagus.
7. Beat the egg whites with the salt until stiff.
8. Mix together the mayonnaise, mustard and lemon juice, then fold into the egg whites. Spoon over the asparagus and sauce.
9. Bake in a 300°F (150°C) oven for 20 minutes or until the meringue is slightly browned.

Serves 8.

Eggplant Souffle

1 eggplant (about 1 lb)	½ teaspoon freshly ground
1½ teaspoons salt	black pepper
3 tablespoons (45 g) butter	3 egg yolks
1 clove garlic, minced	4 egg whites
2½ tablespoons plain flour	⅛ teaspoon baking powder
1¼ cups (300 ml) milk	
½ cup grated Parmesan cheese	

1. Bake the eggplant in a 400°F (200°C) oven for about 45 minutes or until tender. Remove from oven and cool. Cut in half and scoop out the pulp. Drain well then mash and season with the 1½ teaspoons salt.
2. In the top of a double boiler melt the butter with the garlic.
3. Stir in the flour until smooth and cook for one minute over simmering water.
4. Slowly add the milk, stirring constantly, and cook until smooth and thick.
5. Remove from the heat and stir in the Parmesan cheese and eggplant pulp. Add the pepper.
6. Add the egg yolks one at a time, beating well after each addition.
7. Blend the baking powder with the egg whites and beat until stiff but not dry.
8. Gently fold the egg whites into the eggplant mixture.
9. Pour into a well-buttered souffle dish and cook in a 350°F (180°C) oven for about 50 minutes. Serve immediately.

Serves 4.

Potato-Cheese Souffle

2 large potatoes, peeled, cooked and mashed, hot	salt
	freshly ground black pepper
½ cup (125 g) sour cream	½ onion, minced
⅔ cup grated Cheddar cheese	2 teaspoons chopped chives
4 eggs, separated	⅛ teaspoon baking powder

1. Beat together the potatoes and sour cream until light.
2. Add the cheese, egg yolks, salt and pepper to taste, minced onion and chopped chives.
3. Blend the egg whites with the baking powder and beat until stiff but not dry.
4. Gently fold the egg whites into the potato mixture and pour into a well-buttered souffle dish.
5. Bake in a 350°F (180°C) oven for 45 minutes.

Serves 4.

Carrot Souffle

2 cups firmly packed grated
carrots
2 tablespoons (30 g) butter
4 tablespoons water
1 teaspoon salt
2 tablespoons minced
chives

2 teaspoons chopped parsley
5½ tablespoons plain flour
1 cup (250 ml) milk
4 eggs, separated

1. Mix the carrots, butter, water, salt, chives and parsley in a saucepan. Cover and cook over a medium heat about ten minutes or until carrots are tender.
2. Stir in the flour and cook over a low heat for one minute.
3. Slowly add milk, stir constantly until thick and smooth. Remove from heat.
4. Add the egg yolks one at a time, beating well after each addition.
5. Beat the egg whites until they form soft peaks. Gently fold into the carrot mixture.
6. Pour into a buttered souffle dish and bake in a 375°F (190°C) oven for about 40 minutes. Serves 4-6.

Asparagus Souffle

4 tablespoons butter
5½ tablespoons plain flour
1½ cups (375 ml) milk
6 egg yolks
2 tablespoons chopped
parsley
4 teaspoons chopped chives
¼ teaspoon dried dill

salt
freshly ground black pepper
¼ cup grated Parmesan
cheese
1 cup cooked asparagus tips,
cut in small pieces
⅛ teaspoon baking powder
8 egg whites

1. Melt the butter in the top of a double boiler over simmering water.
2. Stir in the flour and cook for one minute.
3. Slowly add the milk, stirring constantly, and cook until smooth and thick.
4. Remove from the heat and, beating constantly, add the egg yolks one at a time.
5. Add the herbs, salt and pepper to taste, cheese and asparagus tips.
6. Combine the baking powder with the egg whites and beat until stiff but not dry.
7. Gently fold into the asparagus mixture.
8. Pour into a well-buttered souffle dish and bake in a 350°F (180°C) oven for about 45 minutes or until set. Serves 6.

Pepper and Cheese Omelette

10 eggs
salt and pepper
4 tablespoons water
1 cup grated Parmesan
  cheese

4 teaspoons (20 g) butter
1 cup grated Gruyere cheese
1 red or green pepper, thinly
  sliced

1. Lightly beat the eggs with salt and pepper to taste and the water.
2. Mix in the Parmesan cheese.
3. Melt the butter in a frypan and pour in the beaten eggs. Cook until almost set over a low heat.
4. Sprinkle on the grated Gruyere cheese and pepper.
5. Place under a hot grill and cook for a few minutes or until the cheese is melted.
6. Remove from the pan, fold over and serve immediately.

Serves 4.

Apple and Cheese Omelette

10 eggs
½ cup grated Parmesan
  cheese
4 tablespoons water
salt and pepper

2 cooking apples, peeled and
  sliced
4 tablespoons (60 g) butter
½ cup crumbled blue cheese

1. Lightly beat together the eggs, Parmesan cheese, water and salt and pepper to taste.
2. Melt half the butter in a frypan and saute the apple slices until heated through. Remove from pan and keep warm.
3. Melt the remaining butter and pour in the egg mixture. Cover and cook until set but not dry.
4. Remove the omelette from the pan and arrange the apples on half. Sprinkle on the blue cheese and fold over. Serve immediately.

Serves 4.

Vegetable Curry

1 lb (500 g) green beans, cut into pieces
2 medium potatoes, peeled and diced
½ lb (250 g) carrots, sliced
⅓ cup (85 g) butter
2 teaspoons cumin seeds.
1½ teaspoons salt

2 teaspoons mustard seeds
2 teaspoons turmeric
1 teaspoon ground coriander
½ teaspoon cayenne
2½ tablespoons lemon juice
1 cup (250 g) yogurt
1 cup fresh peas

1. Mix together the green beans, potatoes and carrots and put into a saucepan with enough water to just cover. Bring to a boil. Reduce heat, cover and cook for five minutes. Remove from heat but do not drain.
2. Heat the butter in a large saucepan. Add the spices and gently cook for two minutes.
3. Add the vegetables with their liquid and the lemon juice. Mix well.
4. Bring to a boil, then add the yogurt and the peas. Reduce the heat and cook over a gentle heat for 30 minutes.

Serves 6.

Cauliflower Curry

2 lb (1 kg) cauliflower
¼ cup (65 g) butter
½ teaspoon ginger
½ teaspoon salt
½ teaspoon turmeric
¼ teaspoon cayenne
½ teaspoon coriander
½ teaspoon mustard seeds

½ teaspoon cumin seeds
2 cloves garlic, minced
⅔ cup (165 ml) water
½ lb (250 g) shelled peas
2½ tablespoons chopped parsley
3 medium tomatoes, chopped

1. Cut the cauliflower into flowerets.
2. Melt the butter in a large frypan and stir in all the spices. Cook gently for two minutes.
3. Add the cauliflower and the water and mix well.
4. Cover and cook over a low heat until the cauliflower is almost tender.
5. Stir in the peas and the parsley and cook for five minutes.
6. Add the tomatoes, mix well and cook only until the tomatoes are heated through.

Serves 4-6.

Egg Curry with Dahl

1 lb (500 g) orange lentils
2 medium onions, chopped
3 tablespoons (45 g) butter
curry powder to taste
salt
8-12 eggs

1. Soak the lentils in enough water to cover for two hours.
2. Saute the onions in the butter until transparent.
3. Add the curry powder to the onions and cook for two minutes.
4. Drain the lentils and add to the onions. Mix well.
5. Add enough water to cover the dahl completely and simmer for 30 minutes. Add more water if necessary. Stir in salt to taste towards the end of the cooking.
6. Boil the eggs for nine minutes.
7. Put the dahl in a serving dish or in individual dishes.
8. Shell and halve the eggs and place on top of the dahl.

Serves 4-6.

Carrot Curry

2 lb (1 kg) carrots, sliced
1 cup (250 ml) orange juice
2½ tablespoons lemon juice
water
1½ teaspoons salt
⅓ cup (85 g) butter
1 teaspoon turmeric
2 teaspoons mustard seeds
4 cardamom pods (seeds only)

1 clove garlic, minced
3 teaspoons cumin seeds
¼ teaspoon cayenne
4 whole cloves
1 banana, sliced
4 tablespoons raisins
2 tablespoons cornstarch

1. Combine the carrots, orange juice, lemon juice, salt and enough water to cover. Simmer for about five minutes.
2. In another saucepan, melt the butter and stir in all the spices. Cook over a low heat for two minutes.
3. Add the carrots with the liquid, the banana and raisins. Cover and simmer for 30 minutes.
4. Mix the cornstarch with a little of the liquid from the curry, then stir into the curry. Heat for a few minutes.

Serves 4-6.

Vegetable Pie

Pastry:
2 cups plain flour
½ teaspoon salt
½ cup (125 g) butter
cold water

Filling:
1 stalk celery, sliced
1 carrot, cooked and sliced
¼ lb (125 g) cauliflower, cut
   up and cooked
1 cup peas, cooked

1 cup corn kernels
¼ lb (125 g) green beans, cut
   up and cooked
1 medium onion, chopped
4 teaspoons (20 g) butter
4 teaspoons plain flour
1 cup (250 ml) milk
salt and pepper
1½ tablespoons chopped
   parsley
¼ cup grated cheese

1. Sift the flour and salt. Rub in the butter until the mixture resembles bread crumbs. Add just enough cold water to form a firm dough. Chill for ½ hour. Roll out a little more than half the dough and line a 9-inch (23-cm) pie tin. Bake in a 400°F (200°C) oven for ten minutes.
2. Mix together the celery, carrot, cauliflower, peas, corn and beans.
3. Saute the onion in the butter until golden brown.
4. Stir in the flour until smooth. Cook for one minute.
5. Slowly add the milk, stirring constantly.
6. Add salt and pepper to taste, chopped parsley and grated cheese. Mix well and cook until smooth and thick.
7. Put the vegetables in prepared pastry. Pour the sauce over the vegetables.
8. Roll out the remaining pastry and cover the pie. Prick a few holes in the top to allow the steam to escape.
9. Bake in a 400°F (200°C) oven for ½ hour.

Serves 4-6.

Asparagus Rolls

1½ lb (750 g) asparagus
6 bread rolls
½ cup (125 ml) melted butter
3 tablespoons (45 g) butter
2½ tablespoons plain flour

2 cups (500 ml) milk
2 teaspoons Parmesan cheese
salt and pepper
¼ teaspoon nutmeg
2½ tablespoons cream

1. Trim the asparagus and cook in boiling salted water until tender. Drain.
2. Cut the bread rolls in half and scoop out the middle.
3. Fry the crusts in the melted butter on both sides until golden brown.
4. Melt the three tablespoons of butter in a saucepan and stir in the flour. Cook for one minute.
5. Slowly add the milk, stirring constantly.
6. Add the Parmesan cheese, salt and pepper to taste, the nutmeg, and the cream.
7. Cut the asparagus into 1-inch (2½-cm) pieces (discarding the tough white ends).
8. Add the asparagus to the sauce and heat through.
9. Pour into the fried rolls and serve immediately.

Serves 4-6.

Zucchini in Casserole

1 lb (500 g) zucchini
5 tablespoons (75 g) butter
2½ tablespoons plain flour
2 cups (500 ml) milk
salt and pepper
¼ teaspoon nutmeg

2 eggs, lightly beaten
2½ tablespoons Parmesan cheese
½ teaspoon salt
¼ teaspoon pepper

1. Cut the zucchini into slices and saute in half the butter until lightly browned.
2. Melt the remaining butter in a saucepan and stir in the flour. Cook for one minute, then slowly add the milk, stirring constantly. Add salt and pepper to taste and nutmeg. Cook until thickened.
3. To this cream sauce, add the eggs, Parmesan cheese, salt and pepper. Mix thoroughly.
4. Gently stir in the fried zucchini.
5. Butter and flour a casserole dish. Pour in the zucchini mixture and put into a pan of hot water.
6. Bake in a 375°F (190°C) oven for 45 minutes. Allow to stand for a few minutes before turning out onto a serving dish.

Serves 4-6.

Pissaladiere

Pastry:
2 cups plain flour
½ teaspoon salt
⅔ cup (165 g) butter
water

Filling:
1½ lb (750 g) onions,
   sliced

½ cup (125 ml) oil
salt and pepper
1 lb (500 g) tomatoes
1 can anchovy fillets
¼ lb (125 g) black olives

1. Sift the flour and salt. Rub in the butter until mixture resembles fine bread crumbs. Add just enough water to form a firm dough. Roll out and line a baking sheet. Pinch the edges to form a case to hold the filling.
2. Saute the onions in the oil over a low heat for 30 minutes. Stir occasionally. Season to taste with salt and pepper.
3. Put the onions on top of the pastry with the oil in which they were cooked.
4. Slice tomatoes and cover onions with the slices. Press down slightly.
5. Arrange the anchovy fillets in a lattice pattern on top of the tomatoes. Place an olive in the centre of each lattice.
6. Sprinkle with a little extra oil and bake in a 375°F (190°C) oven for 30 minutes.

Serves 4-6.

Celery and Almonds

6 cups sliced celery
¼ cup (65 g) butter
1 teaspoon salt
½ teaspoon pepper
¼ teaspoon nutmeg
2½ tablespoons minced spring
   onions

1 cup (115 g) slivered
   almonds
2 teaspoons butter
5 tablespoons dry sherry

1. Saute the celery in the butter with the salt, pepper and nutmeg for two minutes. Cover and cook for another ten minutes.
2. Add the onions, mix well and cook for two minutes.
3. Brown the almonds in the butter, then stir the sherry and cook for two minutes.
4. Pour over the celery and serve immediately.

Serves 6-8.

Mushroom Barley Ring

1½ cups barley
4 cups (1 liter) water
1 teaspoon caraway seeds
1 teaspoon salt
4 tablespoons (60 g) butter
½ lb (250 g) mushrooms,
 sliced
2½ tablespoons chopped
 parsley

1 clove garlic, minced
1 teaspoon salt
¼ teaspoon pepper
¼ teaspoon marjoram
4 tablespoons (60 g) butter
4 tablespoons water

1. Mix together the barley, water, caraway seeds and salt in a saucepan. Bring to a boil. Reduce heat, cover and simmer for about one hour or until tender.
2. Melt four tablespoons butter in a saucepan and add the mushrooms, parsley, garlic, salt, pepper and marjoram. Cook for five minutes.
3. Add the second four tablespoons butter and the water and heat thoroughly.
4. Drain the barley and add to the mushroom mixture.
5. Pour into a well-buttered ring mold, place in a pan of hot water and bake in a 350°F (180°C) oven for 45 minutes.

Serves 6-8.

Baked Soybeans

1½ cups dried soybeans
1 medium onion, chopped
4 tablespoons (60 g) butter
4 tablespoons molasses
1 cup (250 ml) tomato sauce

1½ teaspoons salt
1½ teaspoons dry mustard
2 teaspoons Worcestershire
 sauce
¼ teaspoon pepper

1. Soak the beans overnight in enough water to cover.
2. Cook the beans in the same water (add more to cover, if necessary), covered, for about three hours or until tender. Add more water when necessary. Drain.
3. Mix the cooked beans with the onion, butter, molasses, tomato sauce, salt, mustard, Worcestershire sauce and pepper.
4. Pour into a buttered casserole dish and bake in a 300°F (150°C) oven for ½ hour. Remove cover, stir and bake for another ½ hour.

Serves 6.

Baked Haricot Beans

2 cups dried haricot beans
2 lb (1 kg) tomatoes
1 medium onion, minced
2 cups finely chopped celery
½ cup (125 ml) olive oil
½ cup chopped stuffed olives

1. Soak the beans in enough water to cover overnight.
2. Cook in the same water, covered, until tender. (Add more water if necessary.)
3. Peel the tomatoes and coarsely chop.
4. Mix together the tomatoes, onion, celery and olive oil in a frypan and cook until the celery is tender.
5. Combine the beans and the olives in a buttered casserole dish.
6. Pour the tomato mixture over them and bake, covered, in a 300°F (150°C) for 2-3 hours.

Serves 8.

Lentils with Cheese

1¾ cups lentils
2 cups (500 ml) water
1 bay leaf
2 teaspoons salt
½ teaspoon pepper
⅛ teaspoon marjoram
¼ teaspoon sage
¼ teaspoon thyme
3 medium onions, chopped
2 cloves garlic, minced
1 lb (500 g) tomatoes, chopped
3 medium carrots, sliced
1 stalk celery, sliced
1 green pepper, chopped
4 tablespoons chopped parsley
½ lb (250 g) grated cheese

1. Rinse the lentils in a colander under running water.
2. Mix the lentils with the two cups water, bay leaf, salt, pepper, marjoram, sage, thyme, onion, garlic and tomatoes.
3. Pour the mixture into a shallow baking dish and cover tightly with aluminum foil.
4. Bake in a 375°F (190°C) oven for ½ hour.
5. Uncover and add the carrots and celery. Mix well. Bake until the vegetables are tender — about 40 minutes.
6. Stir in the green pepper and parsley and sprinkle with the grated cheese. Bake uncovered until the cheese melts.

Serves 6-8.

Lentils and Wheat

½ cup lentils
2 cups (500 ml) water
1½ teaspoons salt
4 tablespoons oil
1 medium onion, chopped

½ lb (250 g) mushrooms, sliced
½ cup cracked wheat
yogurt
chopped scallions

1. Mix together the lentils, water and salt in a saucepan. Bring to a boil. Reduce heat and simmer, covered, for 20 minutes.
2. Saute the onion in the oil for two minutes.
3. Add the mushrooms and wheat and cook for five minutes.
4. Add the lentils with the water and bring to a boil. Cover. reduce heat and simmer for 15 minutes or until the wheat is tender.
5. Serve topped with yogurt and chopped scallions.

Serves 4.

Parsnip Pie

Pastry:
1 cup plain flour
½ teaspoon salt
⅓ cup (85 g) butter
cold water

Filling:
1½ lb (750 g) parsnips
4 teaspoons honey

¼ teaspoon ginger
¼ teaspoon nutmeg
4 teaspoons grated lemon rind
½ cup (125 ml) lemon juice
2 egg yolks

1. Sift together the flour and salt. Rub in the butter until the mixture resembles fine bread crumbs. Add just enough cold water to form a firm dough. Roll out and line a 9-inch (23-cm) flan case. Bake in a 400°F (200°C) oven for ten minutes.
2. Boil the parsnips and press through a strainer or puree in an electric blender.
3. Add the honey, ginger, nutmeg, lemon rind, lemon juice and lightly beaten egg yolks. Mix thoroughly.
4. Pour into the prepared pastry and bake in a 350°F (180°C) oven until set and golden brown—about 35 minutes.

Serves 6.

Paprika Peas

3 lb (1½ kg) fresh peas
1 teaspoon sugar
1 teaspoon salt
water
1 small onion, minced
4 tablespoons (60 g) butter
¼ cup plain flour

1 teaspoon salt
¼ teaspoon pepper
1 teaspoon paprika
½ cup (125 ml) milk
¼ cup (65 ml) cream
½ cup grated cheese

1. Shell and wash the peas and put into a saucepan with the sugar, salt and enough water to cover. Cook for about 20 minutes or until tender. Drain and keep warm.
2. Saute the onion in the butter until golden brown.
3. Stir in the flour and cook over a low heat for one minute.
4. Add the salt, pepper, paprika and milk, stirring constantly.
5. Add the cream and cook until thick and smooth.
6. Put the peas in a baking dish and pour on the sauce.
7. Sprinkle on the grated cheese and put under a hot broiler until golden brown.

Serves 6-8.

Asparagus Vinaigrette

2 lb (1 kg) fresh asparagus
2 teaspoons salt
½ cup (125 ml) oil
5 tablespoons chopped
   parsley
2 hard-boiled eggs, chopped
   finely

½ cup (125 ml) vinegar
2½ tablespoons chopped green
   pepper
2 teaspoons chopped chives
freshly ground black pepper
¼ teaspoon paprika

1. Snap off the tough ends of the stalks. Cook the asparagus in boiling salted water until tender. Drain and cool.
2. Mix together the remaining ingredients.
3. Pour over the cooled asparagus and allow to marinate for ½ hour before serving.

Serves 6.

Mushroom and Tomato Pasties

Pastry:
1½ cups plain flour
¼ teaspoon salt
⅓ cup (85 g) butter
cold water

Filling:
3 tablespoons (45 g) butter
1 clove garlic, minced
2 small onions, chopped
½ lb (250 g) mushrooms, sliced

½ lb (250 g) tomatoes, chopped
2 teaspoons chopped parsley
1 teaspoon chopped chives
1 teaspoon chopped marjoram
1 teaspoon chopped oregano
salt
1 egg, beaten

1. Sift the salt and the flour and rub in the butter until the mixture resembles bread crumbs. Add enough water to form a firm dough. Chill for 30 minutes.
2. Melt the butter and saute the garlic and the onions until the onions are transparent.
3. Add the mushrooms and cook for another five minutes.
4. Stir in the tomatoes, herbs and salt to taste. Cook for three minutes. Drain off any liquid that remains.
5. Roll out the pastry thinly and cut into circles.
6. Put a spoonful of the mixture on one half of the circle. Brush the edges with a little of the beaten egg, fold over and press firmly. Brush the top with beaten egg.
7. Put on a buttered baking tray and bake in a 425°F (220°C) oven for about 20 minutes.

Serves 4.

Cauliflower Custard

1 large cauliflower	1 teaspoon salt
2 eggs, beaten	½ teaspoon pepper
4 teaspoons (20 ml) melted butter	1 cup (250 ml) cream

1. Trim and wash the cauliflower and cook in boiling salted water until tender.
2. Drain the cauliflower and chop finely.
3. Mix together the egg, butter, salt, pepper and cream.
4. Add the cauliflower and mix well.
5. Pour into a well-buttered casserole dish and bake in a 325°F (160°C) oven for about 45 minutes or until set.

Serves 6-8.

Asparagus Ring

1½ lb (750 g) fresh asparagus	2½ tablespoons plain flour
1½ teaspoons salt	1 teaspoon salt
¼ teaspoon pepper	¼ teaspoon pepper
¼ teaspoon paprika	2 cups (500 ml) milk
2 eggs, separated	½ cup (125 ml) cream
3 tablespoons (45 g) butter	bread crumbs

1. Snap off the tough ends of the asparagus stalks. Cook in boiling salted water until tender. Drain and chop.
2. Mix the asparagus with the salt, pepper, paprika and well-beaten egg yolks.
3. Melt the butter in a saucepan and stir in the flour, salt and pepper. Cook over a low heat for one minute.
4. Slowly add the milk and cream, stirring constantly until smooth and thick.
5. Pour the white sauce to the asparagus mixture and blend thoroughly.
6. Beat the egg whites until stiff and gently fold into the mixture.
7. Sprinkle the bread crumbs on a well-buttered ring mold.
8. Pour in the asparagus mixture and place in a pan of warm water.
9. Bake in a 350°F (180°C) oven for 45 minutes.

Serves 6-8.

Broccoli Supreme

1½ lb (750 g) broccoli	2 teaspoons prepared horseradish
3 tablespoons (45 g) butter	salt and pepper
2½ tablespoons plain flour	¼ teaspoon thyme
½ cup (125 g) sour cream	

1. Trim the broccoli and cook in boiling salted water until tender. Drain and reserve ½ cup of the liquid.
2. Melt the butter in a saucepan and stir in the flour. Cook over a low heat for one minute.
3. Slowly add the reserved broccoli, stirring constantly until thick and smooth.
4. Add the sour cream, horseradish, salt and pepper to taste and thyme.
5. Put the broccoli on a serving dish and pour the sauce over it. Serve immediately.

Serves 6.

Dilled Green Beans

1 cup chopped onions	¼ teaspoon pepper
5 tablespoons (75 g) butter	1½ tablespoons chopped fresh dill
2 lb (1 kg) fresh beans	2 hard-boiled eggs, chopped
1 teaspoon salt	

1. Saute the onions in the butter until golden brown.
2. Meanwhile, cook the prepared beans in boiling salted water until just tender. Do not overcook. Drain.
3. Add the beans to the onions with the salt, pepper and dill. Mix well and cook for two minutes.
4. Put the beans on a serving dish and top with chopped eggs.

Serves 6.

Green Beans with Sour Cream

1½ lb (750 g) green beans
½ lb (250 g) mushrooms, sliced
3 tablespoons (45 g) butter

1 cup (250 g) sour cream
1 teaspoon salt
chopped parsley

1. Trim the beans and cook in boiling salted water until tender. Drain and keep warm.
2. Saute the mushrooms in the butter for five minutes.
3. Add the sour cream and salt.
4. Put the beans on a serving dish and pour the mushrooms and sour cream over them.
5. Sprinkle with chopped parsley and serve immediately.

Serves 6.

Tomato Pudding

3½ cups sieved tomatoes
½ teaspoon salt
¼ teaspoon pepper
1 cup brown sugar
8 slices bread, cubed
⅓ cup (85 g) butter

1. Mix together the sieved tomatoes, salt, pepper and sugar in a saucepan and bring to a boil.
2. Place the bread cubes in a well-buttered casserole dish.
3. Melt the butter and pour over the bread. Toss to mix.
4. Pour the hot tomato mixture over the buttered bread cubes and bake uncovered in a 350°F (180°C) oven for 45 minutes.

Serves 4-6.

Green Beans with Cheese Sauce

1½ lb (750 g) green beans   ¼ teaspoon thyme
4 tablespoons (60 g) butter   ¼ teaspoon marjoram
1 small onion, chopped   1 teaspoon salt
½ lb (250 g) mushrooms   1 cup (250 ml) milk
4 tablespoons plain flour   1 cup grated Swiss cheese
¼ teaspoon pepper   4 tablespoons sherry

1. Trim the beans and cook in boiling salted water until just tender. Drain and keep warm.
2. Melt the butter in a frypan and saute the onion until transparent.
3. Add the sliced mushrooms and cook for another five minutes.
4. Stir in the flour, pepper, thyme, marjoram and salt and cook over a low heat for one minute.
5. Slowly add the milk, stirring constantly until smooth and thick. Remove from heat.
6. Add the cheese and sherry and stir until the cheese is melted.
7. Add the beans, mix well and pour into a shallow casserole dish.
8. Bake, uncovered, in a 400°F (200°C) oven for ½ hour.

Serves 6.

Cauliflower Polonaise

1 large cauliflower   2½ tablespoons minced parsley
5 tablespoons (75 g) butter   ½ teaspoon salt
2½ tablespoons dried bread   ¼ teaspoon pepper
   crumbs   2 hard-boiled eggs, chopped
1 teaspoon lemon juice

1. Cook the cauliflower whole in boiling salted water until tender. Drain and keep warm.
2. Melt the butter and add the bread crumbs. Stir until brown.
3. Combine the lemon juice, parsley, salt and pepper. Add to the bread crumbs and mix well.
4. Pour this mixture over the cauliflower and sprinkle with chopped eggs.

Serves 6-8.

Carrot Ring

1 cup (250 g) butter
¾ cup brown sugar
1½ cups grated carrots
2 egg yolks, beaten
2½ tablespoons lemon juice
4 teaspoons grated lemon
   rind

1½ cups cake flour
½ teaspoon baking soda
1 teaspoon cinnamon
½ teaspoon nutmeg
1 teaspoon baking powder
2 egg whites, stiffly beaten

1. Cream together the butter and sugar.
2. Add the carrots, egg yolks, lemon juice and lemon rind. Mix thoroughly.
3. Add the flour, baking soda, cinnamon, nutmeg, and baking powder which have been sifted twice.
4. Gently fold in the egg whites.
5. Pour into a well-buttered and floured ring mold and bake in a 350°F (180°C) oven for about 45 minutes.

Serves 6.

Green Beans Au Gratin

1½ lb (750 g) green beans
¾ cup (185 ml) milk
3 tablespoons (45 g) butter
¾ cup grated cheese
salt

¼ teaspoon paprika
⅛ teaspoon cayenne
bread crumbs
butter

1. Chop the beans finely and mix the milk, butter, ½ cup cheese and the seasonings.
2. Pour into a buttered baking dish and bake in a 350°F (180°C) oven for one hour. Stir occasionally during the baking.
3. Ten minutes before the end of the cooking time, sprinkle with the remaining cheese and bread crumbs. Dot with butter and bake until golden brown.

Serves 6.

Broccoli Ring

2 lb (1 kg) broccoli	1 cup (250 ml) cream
1 clove garlic	4 eggs, separated
3 tablespoons (45 g) butter	salt
2½ tablespoons plain flour	freshly ground black pepper

1. Cook the broccoli in boiling salted water with the garlic clove until tender. Drain, remove the garlic and chop the broccoli into small pieces.
2. Melt the butter in a saucepan and stir in the flour. Cook over a low heat for one minute.
3. Slowly add the cream, stirring constantly. Cook until smooth and thick.
4. Beat the egg yolks and add to the white sauce with the broccoli.
5. Beat the egg whites until stiff and fold into the broccoli mixture. Season to taste with salt and pepper.
6. Pour into a buttered and floured ring tin.
7. Place in a pan of boiling water and bake in a 350°F (180°C) oven for ½ hour.

Serves 6.

Tomatoes Vertis

8 large tomatoes	4 tablespoons (60 g) butter
2 medium carrots	1 egg, beaten
1 medium green pepper	1 cup dried bread crumbs
1 medium onion	½ cup (125 ml) milk
2 stalks celery	½ teaspoon salt
2 cups chopped spinach	¼ teaspoon black pepper
1½ tablespoons parsley	grated cheese

1. Cut a thin slice from the top of the tomatoes. Scoop out the pulp.
2. Chop all the vegetables coarsely and put through a mincer.
3. Melt the butter, add the vegetables and simmer until they are brown.
4. Add the egg, bread crumbs, milk, salt and pepper. Mix well, then fill the tomatoes.
5. Sprinkle with the grated cheese and put in a buttered baking dish.
6. Bake in a 400°F (200°C) oven for about 20 minutes or until the tomatoes are tender.

Serves 8.

Baked Tomatoes with Cucumbers

2 cucumbers	salt and pepper
1½ tablespoons grated onion	4 large tomatoes
4 teaspoons lemon juice	bread crumbs
⅓ cup (85 g) butter	chopped parsley
⅓ cup (85 ml) water	butter

1. Peel and dice the cucumbers.
2. Mix together with the onion, lemon juice, butter, water and salt and pepper to taste. Cook for five minutes.
3. Cut a slice off the top of the tomatoes and scoop out the pulp. Turn the tomatoes upside down to drain for 15 minutes.
4. Fill the tomatoes with the cooked cucumber mixed with the tomato pulp.
5. Sprinkle with bread crumbs and chopped parsley and dot with butter.
6. Bake in a 400°F (200°C) oven for 20 minutes or until the tomatoes are tender and the crumbs golden brown.

Serves 4.

Devilled Tomatoes

6 medium tomatoes	2 hard-boiled egg yolks
salt and pepper	1 egg, lightly beaten
plain flour	4 tablespoons vinegar
⅔ cup (165 g) butter	½ teaspoon salt
1½ teaspoons dry mustard	cayenne

1. Cut the tomatoes into thick slices.
2. Season a little flour with salt and pepper and coat the tomato slice.
3. Melt two tablespoons of the butter in a frypan and saute the tomatoes for five minutes.
4. In the top of a double boiler mix together the remaining butter, mustard, finely chopped egg yolks, the egg, vinegar, salt and a pinch of cayenne.
5. Put over hot water and cook, stirring constantly, until smooth and thick.
6. Put the tomatoes on a warm serving dish and pour the sauce over them. Serve immediately.

Serves 4-6.

47

Mashed Carrots

2 lb (1 kg) carrots
½ lb (250 g) potatoes
4 tablespoons (60 g) butter
salt and pepper
1 medium onion, chopped
2½ tablespoons chopped
   parsley

1. Peel the carrots, cut into chunks and cook in enough boiling salted water to cover until very tender. Drain but reserve the liquid, then mash.
2. Peel the potatoes and cook in boiling salted water until tender. Drain and mash.
3. Mix together the carrots and potatoes.
4. Measure ⅔ cup (165 ml) of the carrots liquid and beat into the mashed carrots with half the butter and salt and pepper to taste. Put into serving dish.
5. Saute the onion in the remaining butter until golden.
6. Pour the onion and butter over the carrots mixture and sprinkle with chopped parsley.

Serves 6.

Creamed Carrots

2 lb (1 kg) carrots
½ cup (125 ml) water
3 tablespoons (45 g) butter
2½ tablespoons plain flour

1½ cups (375 ml) milk
salt
½ teaspoon sugar
nutmeg

1. Peel the carrots and cut into cubes.
2. Put into the saucepan with the ½ cup water and cook, covered, for about ten minutes. Strain if necessary.
3. In another saucepan melt the butter and stir in the flour. Cook for one minute over a low heat.
4. Slowly add the milk, stirring constantly, until smooth and thick.
5. Add the carrots, salt to taste and the sugar. Heat through and serve sprinkled with nutmeg.

Serves 6.

Creamed Beets

2 lb (1 kg) beets
3 tablespoons (45 g) butter
4 tablespoons plain flour
1¼ cups (300 ml) water
2½ tablespoons lemon juice

1 teaspoon crushed bay
   leaves
4 teaspoons sugar
salt

1. Wash the beets thoroughly being careful not to break the skin. Cut off the leaves but leave on the roots. Cook in boiling salted water until tender. Peel and cut into cubes.
2. Melt the butter in a saucepan and stir in the flour. Cook over a low heat for one minute.
3. Mix the water with the lemon juice and slowly add to the butter and flour, stirring constantly. Cook until thick and smooth.
4. Stir in the bay leaves, sugar and salt to taste.
5. Add the beets, mix well and cook for another five minutes.

Serves 4-6.

Rice with Vegetables

4 tablespoons (60 g) butter
1 medium onion, chopped
1 clove garlic, minced
1 medium carrot, diced
2 stalks celery, chopped
1 cup rice

1½ cups (375 ml) stock
2½ tablespoons chopped
   parsley
salt
grated Parmesan cheese

1. Melt the butter and saute the onion and garlic until the onion is transparent.
2. Add the carrot and celery and cook for another three minutes.
3. Stir in the rice and cook for a few minutes until the rice is well coated with the butter.
4. Heat the stock and mix with the parsley. Pour onto the rice and vegetables, mix a few times then cover tightly and cook over a medium to low heat for 20 minutes. By this time the liquid should all be absorbed and the rice tender. If not, add a little more liquid, cover and cook for another few minutes.
5. Season to taste with salt and sprinkle with cheese before serving.

Serves 4.

Stuffed Cabbage

1 small cabbage
Stuffing:
¼ lb (125 g) bread without crust
1½ cups (375 ml) milk
1 medium onion, chopped
1 clove garlic, minced
¼ lb (125 g) mushrooms, chopped
3 tablespoons (45 g) butter

4 tablespoons grated cheese
½ teaspoon marjoram
½ teaspoon tarragon
2 eggs
salt
4 teaspoons (20 g) butter
1 medium onion
1½ cups (375 ml) stock
2½ tablespoons tomato paste

1. Wash the cabbage well and cook in boiling salted water until tender. Drain and cool.
2. Cut the bread into large cubes and soak in the milk for ½ hour. Mash well or press through a strainer.
3. Saute the onion, garlic and mushrooms in the butter for five minutes.
4. Mix in the grated cheese, marjoram, tarragon and lightly beaten eggs. Season to taste with salt.
5. Remove the leaves of the cabbage one by one. Put a couple of spoonfuls of the stuffing onto each leaf and roll them up. Repeat until all the stuffing is used.
6. Place the rolls in the buttered baking dish.
7. Saute the onion in the butter until golden brown.
8. Mix the stock with the tomato paste and combine with the sauteed onion.
9. Pour over the stuffed cabbage and bake in a 350°F (180°C) oven for about one hour.

Serves 4-6.

Potatoes with Herbs

1 medium onion, chopped	2 teaspoons chopped
4 tablespoons (60 g) butter	marjoram
1½ lb (750 g) potatoes	2 teaspoons chopped
1½ cups (375 ml) vegetable	oregano
stock or water	2 teaspoons chopped thyme
salt	(or any combination of fresh
1½ tablespoons chopped	herbs)
parsley	

1. Saute the onion in the butter for three minutes.
2. Peel the potatoes and slice thickly. Add to the onion and gently fry for five minutes, turning over and stirring occasionally.
3. Pour the vegetable stock or water over the potatoes, season to taste with salt, cover and cook for 20 minutes.
4. Sprinkle on the chopped herbs, cover and cook for another ten minutes.

Serves 4-6.

Baked Tomatoes

6 large tomatoes
3 eggs
2½ tablespoons plain flour
4 tablespoons cream
2½ tablespoons parsley
salt and pepper

1. Cut the top off the tomatoes and carefully scoop out the pulp.
2. Lightly beat the eggs and mix together with the flour, cream, parsley and the tomato pulp.
3. Season to taste with salt and pepper.
4. Spoon the mixture into the tomato shell.
5. Place the tomatoes in a well-buttered baking dish and cook in a 400°F (200°C) oven for 15-20 minutes.

Serves 6.

Haricot Bean Stew

1 cup haricot beans	1 stalk celery, sliced
3 tablespoons (45 g) butter	2½ tablespoons chopped
2 medium onions, chopped	parsley
1 clove garlic, minced	salt
2 potatoes, peeled and cubed	freshly ground black pepper
2 medium carrots, cubed	chopped chives

1. Soak the beans in enough water to cover for several hours. Cook in the same water until tender. Do not drain.
2. Saute the onions and garlic in the butter until golden brown.
3. Add the potatoes and carrots and cook for ten minutes.
4. Stir in the celery and parsley and cook for another five minutes.
5. Mix the vegetables with the beans and cook until all the vegetables are soft.
6. Season to taste with salt and pepper. Sprinkle with chopped chives.

Serves 4-6.

Rice Croquettes

1 medium onion, chopped	2½ tablespoons plain flour
3 tablespoons (45 g) butter	⅓ cup grated cheese
1½ tablespoons chopped	1 large egg, beaten
parsley	dried bread crumbs
1 cup rice	oil for frying
1½ cups (375 ml) hot water	

1. Saute the onion in the butter until transparent.
2. Add the parsley and the rice and stir until the rice is well coated with the butter and golden brown.
3. Add the hot water, stir a few times, cover and cook over a low to medium heat for 20 minutes. The water should be absorbed and the rice tender after this time. If the rice is not yet cooked, add a little more water and cook for a few more minutes. If the water has not all been absorbed, cook for a few minutes uncovered, stirring frequently. Cool the rice mixture completely.
4. Mix the flour and cheese with the rice and form into croquettes.
5. Dip them into the beaten egg, then into the dried bread crumbs coating them thoroughly.
6. Heat the oil and either shallow or deep fry until golden brown.

Serves 4.

Mushroom Pie

Pastry:
2 cups plain flour
½ teaspoon salt
½ cup (125 g) butter
cold water

Filling:
3 medium onions, chopped
5 tablespoons (75 g) butter

1½ lb (750 g) mushrooms
1 bay leaf
4 tablespoons plain flour
1¼ cups (300 ml) milk
salt
1 cup diced potatoes, cooked
2½ tablespoons chopped parsley

1. Sift together the flour and salt. Rub in the butter until the mixture resembles fine bread crumbs. Add enough water to form a firm dough. Chill for ½ hour. Roll out a little more than half the dough and line a 9-inch (23-cm) pie tin. Bake in a 400°F (200°C) oven for ten minutes.
2. Saute the onions in half the butter until transparent.
3. Wipe the mushrooms with a damp cloth and cut into slices. Add to the onions and cook with the bay leaf for five minutes. Strain and reserve the liquid.
4. Melt the remaining butter in a saucepan and stir in the flour. Cook for one minute over a low heat.
5. Slowly add the milk, stirring constantly. Add the reserved liquid and stir until smooth and thick.
6. Season to taste with salt.
7. Add the mushrooms, onions and potatoes. Heat thoroughly.
8. Pour into the prepared pastry and sprinkle with the chopped parsley.
9. Roll out the remaining pastry and cover the pie. Prick a few holes in the top to allow the steam to escape.
10. Bake in a 400°F (200°C) oven for 45 minutes.

Serves 4-6.

Nut Casserole

½ lb (250 g) tomatoes, sliced
1 medium onion, chopped
½ lb (250 g) grated roasted
    nuts (not peanuts)
3 eggs

2 teaspoons chopped parsley
2 teaspoons chopped
    marjoram
salt and pepper

1. Mix together the tomatoes, onion and grated nuts.
2. Beat the eggs with the parsley, marjoram and salt and pepper to taste.
3. Mix the egg mixture with the nut mixture beating well.
4. Pour the mixture into a well-buttered casserole dish.
5. Bake in a 400°F (200°C) oven for about 35 minutes.
6. Turn out onto a hot serving dish and serve with gravy if desired. May also be served cold.

Serves 4.

Lentil Patties

½ lb (125 g) red lentils
4 cups (1 liter) water
3 cups dried bread crumbs
2 eggs
salt
1½ tablespoons chopped
    parsley

2 teaspoons chopped fresh
    marjoram
2½ tablespoons milk
oil for frying

1. Soak the lentils in the four cups of water overnight. Cook in the same water until soft. Drain if necessary.
2. Mix together the lentils, two cups of bread crumbs, one egg, salt to taste, parsley and marjoram. Set aside for 30 minutes.
3. Form the lentil mixture into patties.
4. Beat together the remaining egg and the milk.
5. Dip the patties first into the egg mixture, then coat with the remaining bread crumbs.
6. Fry in the oil until golden brown.

Serves 4.

Nut Rissoles

4 tablespoons (60 g) butter
4 tablespoons plain flour
1¼ cup (300 ml) vegetable
   stock or water
salt
¼ teaspoon marjoram
½ teaspoon thyme

1 cup dried bread crumbs
⅔ cup grated roasted nuts (not
   peanuts)
1 egg
2½ tablespoons milk
oil for frying

1. Melt the butter and stir in the flour until smooth. Cook over a low heat for one minute.
2. Slowly add the vegetable stock or water, salt to taste, marjoram and thyme, stirring constantly until smooth and thick.
3. Remove from heat and stir in ¾ cup of the bread crumbs and the nuts. Allow mixture to cool, then shape into rissoles.
4. Beat the egg with the milk and dip the rissoles into it.
5. Coat the rissoles with the remaining bread crumbs and fry in the oil until golden brown.

Serves 4.

Semolina Gnocchi

2½ cups (625 ml) water
1¼ cups (300 ml) milk
½ teaspoon salt
⅔ cup semolina
2 eggs

½ cup (125 ml) milk
½ cup (125 ml) cream
½ cup grated cheese
butter
nutmeg

1. Heat together the water, milk and salt.
2. Slowly add the semolina, stirring constantly. Cook for 20 minutes.
3. Spread the cooked semolina in a flat dish about ½-inch (1-cm) deep. Allow to cool completely, then cut into cubes.
4. Butter an oven-proof dish and put the semolina squares in it.
5. Lightly beat the eggs and blend with the milk and cream. Pour over the semolina.
6. Sprinkle with grated cheese and dot with butter. Sprinkle on a little nutmeg and bake in a 350°F (180°C) oven for about 40 minutes.

Serves 4.

Spaghetti with Eggs

¼ lb (125 g) spaghetti
1 large green pepper, chopped
1 large onion, chopped
4 tablespoons (60 g) butter

3 eggs
¼ cup (65 ml) milk
½ teaspoon salt
¼ teaspoon black pepper

1. Cook the spaghetti in boiling salted water until tender. Drain.
2. Meanwhile, saute the pepper and onion in two tablespoons of butter until the onion is golden brown.
3. Add the spaghetti and the remaining butter to the pepper and onion mixture and mix well.
4. Beat together the eggs, milk, salt and pepper.
5. Stir into the spaghetti mixture until the eggs are cooked.

Serves 4.

Tomato Cakes

¾ cup rolled oats
⅓ cup (85 ml) water
1½ tablespoons tomato paste
2 medium tomatoes, chopped
1 onion, minced

1 egg, lightly beaten
2 teaspoons chopped parsley
salt and pepper
oil for frying

1. Mix the oats with the water and tomato paste and allow to stand for 15 minutes.
2. Add the tomatoes and onion and mix well.
3. Stir in the egg, parsley and salt and pepper to taste.
4. Form the mixture into small cakes and fry in the oil over a low heat until golden brown.

Serves 4.

Beets Supreme

1 lb (500 g) beets
½ lb (250 g) potatoes
3 tablespoons (45 g) butter or
  bacon fat
2 small onions, chopped
2½ tablespoons plain flour
1¼ cups (300 ml) vegetable
  stock or water
2½ tablespoons lemon juice

2 teaspoons brown sugar
salt
1 bay leaf
2 teaspoons capers
5 tablespoons chopped
  gherkins
2 cooking apples
½ cup (125 g) sour cream
chopped chives

1. Carefully wash the beets and cut off the leaves but not the roots and cook in boiling water for about ½ hour or until soft. Cool, peel and dice.
2. Peel the potatoes and cook in boiling salted water until tender, but not too soft. Cook and dice.
3. Melt the butter or bacon fat and saute the onions until golden brown.
4. Stir in the flour and cook for one minute.
5. Slowly add the vegetable stock or water stirring constantly, until smooth and thick.
6. Add the lemon juice, brown sugar, salt to taste, bay leaf, capers and chopped gherkins. Cook over a low heat for five minutes.
7. Peel and core the apples and cut into small cubes. Add to the white sauce.
8. Pour the sauce over the beets and potatoes, mix well and heat through.
9. Just before serving, remove the bay leaf, stir in the sour cream and sprinkle with the chopped chives.

Serves 4-6.

Duchess Potatoes

2 lb (1 kg) cooked potatoes
2½ tablespoons cream
3 tablespoons (45 g) butter
3 egg yolks
salt
nutmeg

1. Mash the potatoes.
2. Gently heat the cream with the butter until the butter has melted.
3. Mix the butter and cream into the potatoes beating well.
4. Beat the egg yolks lightly and mix into the potatoes.
5. Season to taste with salt and nutmeg.
6. Pour into a well-buttered baking dish, sprinkle with a little nutmeg and bake in a 425°F (220°C) oven until brown.

Serves 6.

Chinese Vegetables

4 stalks celery, sliced
1 lb (500 g) cabbage, coarsely sliced
3 medium onions, sliced
¼ lb (125 g) carrots, sliced
¼ cup (65 ml) oil
1 cup (250 ml) stock
2 teaspoons soy sauce
2½ tablespoons cornstarch
5 tablespoons water
½ lb (250 g) bean sprouts
salt

1. Mix together the celery, cabbage, onions and carrots and saute in the hot oil for five minutes.
2. Stir in the stock and soy sauce and cook for ten minutes.
3. Blend the cornstarch with the water and stir into the vegetables. Cook until tender.
4. Add the bean sprouts and cook until tender.
5. Season to taste with salt and serve immediately.

Serves 4-6.

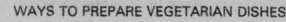

Peppers and Tomatoes

1 medium onion, chopped
2 cloves garlic, minced
2½ tablespoons olive oil
4 teaspoons (20 g) butter
½ lb (250 g) green peppers
½ lb (250 g) red peppers

1 lb (500 g) tomatoes
1 bay leaf
salt
freshly ground black pepper
chopped parsley

1. Saute the onion and garlic in the olive oil and butter until golden brown.
2. Remove the seeds from the peppers and cut into slices.
3. Add the peppers to the onion and cook for five minutes.
4. Quarter the tomatoes and add to the peppers with the bay leaf and salt and pepper to taste. Cover the cook for five to ten minutes.
5. Serve with chopped parsley sprinkled on top.

Serves 4-6.

Creamed Spinach

2 lb (1 kg) spinach
3 tablespoons (45 g) butter
2½ tablespoons plain flour
½ cup (125 ml) vegetable
   stock or water

1 cup (250 ml) cream
salt
freshly ground black pepper
nutmeg

1. Wash the spinach thoroughly several times under running water. Cut out the coarse white stem. Cook in a covered saucepan with no extra water added for about five minutes. Drain. Press through a strainer or pureé in an electric blender.
2. Melt the butter in a saucepan and stir in the flour. Cook over a low heat for one minute.
3. Slowly add the vegetable stock or water, stirring constantly. Remove from heat.
4. Gradually add the cream, stirring constantly. Return to the heat and cook, continuing to stir, until thick and smooth.
5. Season to taste with salt, freshly ground black pepper and nutmeg.
6. Stir the sauce into the spinach and heat thoroughly.

Serves 4.

Fennel Au Gratin

6 fennel plants
butter
½ cup (125 ml) cream
⅔ cup grated cheese

1. Trim the fennel and cut in half lengthwise. Rinse under running water. Cook in enough boiling salted water to cover until tender—15 to 30 minutes.
2. Drain the fennel and place in a well-buttered baking dish.
3. Pour the cream over the fennel and sprinkle with the grated cheese.
4. Dot with butter and bake in a 325°F (160°C) oven until lightly browned.

Serves 6.

Mashed Parsnips

1 lb (500 g) parsnips
½ lb (250 g) potatoes
salt
1 medium onion, chopped
3 tablespoons (45 g) butter
chopped parsley

1. Trim and peel the parsnips and cut into thick slices. Cook in boiling salted water until tender.
2. Peel the potatoes and cut into chunks. Cook in boiling salted water until tender.
3. Mash the parsnips and the potatoes separately, then mix together.
4. Add salt to taste and half the butter and beat until smooth.
5. Saute the onion in the remaining butter until golden brown.
6. Put the parsnips mixture on a serving dish and pour on the onion and butter.
7. Sprinkle with chopped parsley and serve immediately.

Serves 4-6.

Rice with Spinach

3 tablespoons (45 g) butter
1 medium onion, chopped
½ lb (250 g) spinach, chopped
1 cup rice

1½ cups (375 ml) hot water
2½ tablespoons chopped parsley
salt
grated Parmesan cheese

1. Melt the butter in a saucepan and saute the onion until transparent.
2. Add the chopped spinach and cook for another five minutes.
3. Add the rice and stir until the rice is well coated with the butter.
4. Add the hot water, stir a few times, cover and cook over a low to medium heat for 20 minutes. The rice should be tender and the water all absorbed after this time. If the rice is not cooked, add a little more water, cover and cook for a few more minutes. If the rice is tender but the water is not all absorbed, cook over a low heat uncovered for a few minutes.
5. Stir in the chopped parsley and season to taste with salt.
6. Serve sprinkled with Parmesan cheese.

Serves 4.

Haricot Beans and Barley

1 cup haricot beans
5 tablespoons pearl barley
2 medium onions, chopped
3 tablespoons (45 g) butter
salt
chopped parsley

1. Soak the beans in enough water to cover for several hours. Cook in the same water until tender. Drain.
2. Rinse the barley and boil in salted water until soft. Drain.
3. Saute the onions in the butter until golden brown.
4. Mix together the beans, barley and onions. Season to taste with salt and heat through.
5. Sprinkle with chopped parsley and serve immediately.

Serves 4-6.

Carrots with Honey

1 lb (500 g) carrots
1 cup (250 ml) vegetable
  stock or water
salt
2½ tablespoons honey
4 teaspoons (20 g) butter

1. Peel the carrots if necessary and cut into slices.
2. Bring the vegetable stock or water to a boil and add the carrots. Cover and simmer until the carrots are tender. Drain.
3. Season to taste with salt.
4. Stir in the honey and butter until both are melted and the carrots are thoroughly coated.

Serves 4.

Peas with Onions

1½ lb (750 g) shelled fresh
  peas
1 cup (250 ml) water
1½ teaspoons salt
1 teaspoon sugar

1 teaspoon chopped mint
½ lb (250 g) small onions
2 tablespoons (30 g) butter
1¼ cups (300 ml) milk
salt and sugar to taste

1. Put the peas, water, salt, sugar and mint in a saucepan, cover and simmer for about 15 minutes or until the peas are tender. Drain.
2. Peel the onions (leave whole) and cook in the butter until soft. Add a little water if the onions are sticking.
3. Add the onions to the peas with the milk.
4. Season to taste with salt and sugar and heat thoroughly.

Serves 4-6.

Kale with White Sauce

2 lb (1 kg) kale
1 cup (250 ml) vegetable stock or water
4 tablespoons (60 g) butter or bacon fat
1 medium onion, chopped
5 tablespoons plain flour

1¼ cups (300 ml) vegetable stock
1¼ cups (300 ml) cream
salt
¼ teaspoon nutmeg
1 teaspoon sugar

1. Trim the kale and wash thoroughly under running water.
2. **Bring the vegetable stock or the water to a boil and add the kale. Cook until soft. Strain and chop finely.**
3. Melt two tablespoons of the butter or bacon fat in a large saucepan and saute the onion until golden brown.
4. Stir in the flour and cook for one minute.
5. Slowly add first the vegetable stock, then the cream, stirring constantly until smooth and thick.
6. Add the kale, salt to taste, nutmeg and sugar. Mix thoroughly.
7. Add the remaining butter or bacon fat and heat thoroughly, mixing constantly.

Serves 4-6.

Tomatoes and Mushrooms

1 medium onion, chopped
3 tablespoons (45 g) butter
1 clove garlic, minced
1 lb (500 g) tomatoes, havled
1 lb (500 g) mushrooms
salt
freshly ground black pepper
chopped chives

1. Saute the onion in the butter until transparent.
2. Add the garlic and cook until the onion is golden brown.
3. Add the tomatoes and cook for five minutes.
4. Wipe the mushrooms with a damp cloth. Cut in half if large; otherwise leave whole. Add to the tomatoes and cook for ten minutes.
5. Season to taste with salt and pepper. Serve sprinkled with chopped chives.

Serves 4-6.

Leeks Au Gratin

2 lb (1 kg) leeks
3 tablespoons (45 g) butter
4 tablespoons plain flour
½ cup (125 ml) vegetable
   stock or water

1 cup (250 ml) milk
salt
nutmeg
⅔ cup grated cheese

1. Trim the roots and damaged outer leaves. Quarter the leeks and wash thoroughly in running water. Place in a saucepan with about half a cup of water, cover and cook over a medium heat until tender. Drain if necessary. Keep warm.
2. Melt the butter in a saucepan and stir in the flour. Cook over a low heat for one minute.
3. Slowly add the vegetable stock or water, stirring constantly, until smooth.
4. Blend in the milk, continuing to stir, until smooth and thick.
5. Add salt and nutmeg to taste and half the cheese. Stir until the cheese is melted.
6. Butter a baking dish and place the leeks in it.
7. Pour cheese sauce over leeks and sprinkle remaining cheese on top.
8. Bake in a 350°F (180°C) oven for ½ hour. Serve immediately.

Serves 4-6.

Chicory with Mushrooms and Tomatoes

1 lb (500 g) chicory
2½ cups (625 ml) water
2½ tablespoons lemon juice
½ lb (250 g) mushrooms

1 medium onion, chopped
½ lb (250 g) tomatoes
4 tablespoons (60 g) butter
salt and pepper

1. Trim the chicory and cut in half. Wash thoroughly.
2. Boil the water with the lemon juice, then add the chicory and cook for about ten minutes. Drain well.
3. Wipe the mushrooms with a damp cloth and cut in slices.
4. Melt half the butter in a frypan and saute the mushrooms and the onion for five minutes. Keep warm.
5. Heat the remaining butter in a large saucepan and stir in the chicory. Cook over a low heat for ten minutes.
6. Quarter the tomatoes and add to the chicory with salt and pepper to taste. Cook for five minutes.
7. Mix mushrooms and onion with chicory mixture and serve immediately.

Serves 4-6.

Corn on the Cob

6 large or 12 small corncobs
water to cover
¼ cup (65 ml) melted butter
salt

1. Remove the outer leaves and the silk from the cobs. Trim top and stem.
2. Drop the corncobs in boiling salted water (just enough to cover the cobs) and cook for from five to seven minutes.
3. Drain and place on a serving dish.
4. Pour on the melted butter and season with salt to taste.

Serves 6.

Braised Chicory

1 lb (500 g) chicory	10 peppercorns
2½ cups (625 ml) water	salt
2½ tablespoons lemon juice	4 teaspoons cornstarch
2 tablespoons (30 g) bacon fat	2½ tablespoons cold water
1 cup (250 ml) water	1½ tablespoon chopped parsley
1 bay leaf	

1. Trim the chicory and cut in half. Wash thoroughly.
2. Boil the water with the lemon juice, then add the chicory and cook for about ten minutes. Drain well. Put in baking dish.
3. Mix together the bacon fat. water, bay leaf, peppercorns and salt to taste in a saucepan. Bring to a boil. Reduce the heat and simmer for ten minutes. Remove the bay leaf and peppercorns.
4. Blend the cornstarch with the cold water and add to the sauce, stirring constantly. Cook for about five minutes or until smooth and thick.
5. Pour the sauce over the chicory and cook, uncovered, in a 350°F (180°C) oven for 20 minutes.
6. Serve sprinkled with chopped parsley.

Serves 4.

Cabbage with Noodles

1 medium cabbage
½ lb (250 g) noodles
3 medium onions, sliced
4 tablespoons (60 g) butter
salt and pepper

1. Quarter the cabbage and cut away the thicker part of the core.
2. Bring a large saucepan of water to a boil and drop in the quarters of cabbage. Cook until tender. Drain.
3. In another saucepan of boiling salted water, cook the noodles. Cook until tender then drain well and mix in two tablespoons of butter.
4. Saute the onions in the remaining two tablespoons of butter until transparent.
5. Chop cabbage and add onions. Stir over low heat for ten minutes.
6. Mix in the buttered noodles, add salt and pepper to taste and serve immediately.

Serves 6-8.

Baked Chick Peas

1 cup dried chick peas
¼ teaspoon baking soda
½ lb (250 g) tomatoes
2 medium green peppers, sliced
2 medium onions, sliced
¼ cup (65 ml) oil
2 cloves garlic, minced

2 teaspoons chopped sweet basil
2 teaspoons chopped tarragon
1½ tablespoons chopped parsley
salt and pepper

1. Soak the chick peas in water to cover with the baking soda. Drain and rinse. Cover with fresh water and cook for about one hour, covered.
2. Dip the tomatoes into boiling water for 30 seconds then peel and chop.
3. Saute the green peppers and onions in the oil for three minutes.
4. Add the garlic, sweet basil, tarragon, parsley and the chopped tomatoes. Cook over a low heat for five minutes.
5. Drain the chick peas and mix with the tomato mixture.
6. Butter a casserole dish and pour the mixture into it. Cover and bake in a 325°F (160°C) oven for one hour.

Serves 4-6.

Stuffed Eggplants

3 small eggplants
2 green peppers, diced
⅓ cup (85 ml) oil
salt and pepper
2 medium onions, chopped
2 cloves garlic, minced
1½ tablespoons chopped
  parsley
4 medium tomatoes, chopped

Topping:
1 cup chopped walnuts
4 tablespoons wheatgerm
½ cup grated Parmesan
  cheese
3 tablespoons (45 ml)
  melted butter
cream

1. Cut the eggplants into half lengthwise and carefully scoop out the flesh. (Don't scoop too close to the skin.) Dice the flesh into large pieces.
2. Saute the eggplant and the peppers in half the oil until the eggplant begins to soften. Season to taste with salt and pepper.
3. Divide this mixture into six portions and press into the six eggplant skins.
4. Heat the rest of the oil and saute the onions and the garlic until the onions are transparent.
5. Add the parsley and the tomatoes and mix well. Cook over a low heat for ten minutes. Spoon the mixture over the eggplant mixture. Press down.
6. Mix together the chopped walnuts, the wheatgerm and the Parmesan cheese. Add the melted butter and enough cream to make a soft paste. Spread on top of each eggplant half.
7. Put the eggplants in a buttered shallow baking dish. Bake in a 350°F (180°C) oven for 45 minutes.

Serves 6.

Baked Spinach

2 lb (1 kg) fresh spinach
2 medium onions, chopped
1 clove garlic, minced
2½ tablespoons oil
butter

2 eggs, beaten
1 cup grated Parmesan
  cheese
salt and pepper

1. Thoroughly wash the spinach and cut out the coarse white stem. Drain.
2. Saute the onions and the garlic in the oil until the onion is transparent.
3. Add the spinach and cover tightly. When the spinach has wilted, stir to blend with the onion and garlic. Recover and cook for another three minutes.
4. Put the spinach in a buttered baking dish.
5. Combine the eggs with half the Parmesan cheese. Season to taste with salt and pepper and pour the mixture on top of the spinach.
6. Sprinkle on the remaining Parmesan cheese and dot with butter.
7. Bake in a 375°F (190°C) oven, uncovered, for about 15 minutes.

Serves 4.

Stuffed Tomatoes

8 large tomatoes
4 tablespoons chopped fresh
  basil
5 tablespoons chopped
  parsley
3 cloves garlic, minced
1½ tablespoons chopped fresh
  marjoram

salt
freshly ground black pepper
1½ cups dried bread crumbs
4 spring onions, chopped
oil
lemon wedges

1. Cut an opening in the top of each tomato. Carefully scoop out the pulp. Invert the tomatoes and allow to drain for 15 minutes.
2. Mix together the basil, parsley, garlic, marjoram, salt and pepper to taste, the bread crumbs and onions.
3. Add the tomato pulp and mix well.
4. Spoon this mixture into the drained tomato shells.
5. Place the tomatoes in an oiled baking dish.
6. Cover and bake in a 350°F (180°C) oven for 30 minutes. Remove the cover and bake for another ten minutes.
7. Serve hot with lemon wedges.

Serves 8.

Potatoes with Cheese

6 large potatoes, peeled, boiled and cubed
1 lb (500 g) cottage cheese
1¼ cups (300 g) sour cream
2 cloves garlic, minced

1½ teaspoons salt
2 medium onions, minced
1 cup grated cheese
paprika
1½ tablespoons chopped chives

1. Mix together the cottage cheese, sour cream, garlic, salt and onions.
2. Add the cubed potatoes and mix gently but thoroughly.
3. Pour into a buttered casserole dish.
4. Sprinkle the grated cheese on top. Add a little paprika.
5. Bake in a 350°F (180°C) oven for about 1½ hours.
6. Sprinkle with chopped chives and serve hot.

Serves 6-8.

Stuffed Vine Leaves

⅓ cup uncooked brown rice
1 lb (500 g) zucchini
2 medium onions, chopped
⅓ cup (85 ml) oil
4 medium tomatoes, chopped

1½ tablespoons lemon juice
2 teaspoons oregano
salt and pepper
1 can (1 lb) vine leaves

1. Cook the rice in boiling water until tender. Drain.
2. Wash the zucchini well and chop finely without peeling.
3. Saute the zucchini and the onions in the oil until the onions are transparent.
4. Add the tomatoes, lemon juice, oregano and salt and pepper to taste. Mix well.
5. Stir in the rice and add more salt and pepper if necessary.
6. Carefully separate the vine leaves and pour a spoonful of the mixture in each one. Roll tightly.
7. If you have any leaves left over after using all the filling, line a baking dish with them. Otherwise oil the baking dish. Arrange the stuffed vine leaves in the baking dish closely together. Pour a little water over them and cover tightly.
8. Bake in a 350°F (180°C) oven for 30 minutes.

Serves 6-8.

Soybean Casserole

1 cup dried soybeans
¼ cup (65 g) butter
1 medium onion, minced
½ teaspoon thyme
½ teaspoon dill
3 teaspoons dried parsley
2 cloves garlic, minced

½ teaspoon black pepper
½ lb (250 g) tomatoes
½ lb (250 g) zucchini
½ cup grated Parmesan
    cheese
butter

1. Wash the soybeans well and soak overnight in enough salted water to cover.
2. Add more water and cook for about three hours or until the beans are tender. Drain but reserve 1¼ cups (300 ml) of the liquid.
3. Saute the onion in the butter until transparent.
4. Add the thyme, dill, parsley, garlic and pepper. Mix well and saute for three minutes.
5. Stir in the beans and the reserved liquid and simmer for ten minutes.
6. Butter a casserole dish and spoon in half the bean mixture.
7. Wash and slice the tomatoes and zucchini. Place on top of the beans and sprinkle with the Parmesan cheese.
8. Spoon on the remaining beans and dot with a little butter.
9. Bake in a 300°F (150°C) oven for two hours.

Serves 4-6.

Eggs Florentine with Mornay Sauce

3 lb (1½ kg) spinach
2½ tablespoons plain flour
⅔ cup (165 ml) cream
salt and pepper

Mornay Sauce:
4 tablespoons (60 g) butter
4 tablespoons plain flour
2½ cups (625 ml) milk

2 teaspoons prepared
  mustard
½ cup grated cheese
4 tablespoons Parmesan
  cheese
salt and pepper
¼ teaspoon nutmeg
6 eggs

1. Wash the spinach thoroughly and cook in a covered saucepan with no extra water added until tender. Drain well. Return to the saucepan.
2. Stir in the flour and cream and simmer over a low heat until all the liquid is absorbed. Season to taste with salt and pepper. Keep warm.
3. Melt the butter and stir in the flour. Cook for one minute.
4. Slowly add the milk, stirring constantly. Cook until thickened.
5. Add the mustard, cheeses, salt and pepper to taste and the nutmeg. Cook over a low heat until smooth.
6. Poach the eggs and keep warm.
7. Put the spinach in a shallow baking dish. Drain the eggs and lay on top. Pour the Mornay Sauce over the eggs.
8. Put the dish under a hot broiler to brown.

Serves 6.

Baked Soybean Croquettes

1 cup dried soybeans
1 medium onion, minced
2 cloves garlic, minced
5 scallions, chopped
½ cup (125 g) butter
5 tablespoons plain flour
1¼ cups (300 ml) milk, warm
½ teaspoon marjoram

½ teaspoon thyme
1½ tablespoons chopped
  parsley
5 tablespoons wheatgerm
salt and pepper
1 egg, beaten
bread crumbs

1. Soak the soybeans in salted water overnight. Add more water and simmer for three hours or until the beans are tender, adding more water when necessary. Drain. Sieve the beans through a strainer.
2. Mix together the onion, garlic and scallions. Saute in half the butter until the onion is transparent.
3. Melt the rest of the butter in a small saucepan. Stir in the flour and cook for one minute. Slowly add the milk, stirring constantly, until thickened.
4. Mix the white sauce with the onions.
5. Pound together the marjoram, thyme and parsley.
6. Combine the soybean puree, the white sauce with the onions, the herbs, wheatgerm and salt and pepper to taste.
7. Shape the soybean mixture into croquettes. Dip first in the beaten egg and then into the bread crumbs.
8. Place in a buttered shallow baking dish and bake in a 400°F (200°C) oven for ½ hour.

Serves 4-6.

Green Gnocchi

1 lb (500 g) spinach
2 lb (1 kg) potatoes
2 egg yolks
3 tablespoons Parmesan
  cheese
½ teaspoon salt

½ cup plain flour
3 quarts boiling water
4 tablespoons salt
melted butter
4 tablespoons Parmesan
  cheese

1. Wash the spinach several times in cold water. Cook in a covered saucepan with no added water until tender. Drain, squeeze dry and strain.
2. Peel the potatoes and cook in boiling salted water until tender. Drain and mash.
3. Mix together the spinach, potatoes, egg yolks, the 3 tablespoons Parmesan cheese, salt and flour.
4. Roll on a floured board in long thin fingers and cut into 2-inch (5-cm) pieces.
5. Add the four tablespoons of salt to the boiling water and cook the gnocchi about 10 pieces at a time until they rise to the top. Remove with a strainer and repeat until all the gnocchi are cooked.
6. Place in a serving dish and sprinkle with melted butter and Parmesan cheese.

(These are delicious served with home-made tomato sauce.)

Serves 4.

Leek Tart

Pastry:
1 cup plain flour
½ teaspoon salt
⅓ cup (85 g) butter
cold water

Filling:
6 leeks, finely sliced

3 tablespoons (45 g) butter
2 eggs
1 egg yolk
salt and pepper
1¼ cups (300 ml) milk
¼ cup Parmesan cheese
¼ teaspoon nutmeg

1. Sift together the flour and salt. Rub in the butter until the mixture resembles fine bread crumbs. Add just enough water to form a firm dough. Roll out and line a 8-inch (20-cm) flan case. Bake in a 400°F (200°C) oven for ten minutes.
2. Saute the leeks in the butter until soft.
3. In a bowl, beat together the eggs and milk. Season to taste with salt and pepper.
4. Add the leeks, the cheese and the nutmeg. Mix well.
5. Pour into the prepared pastry and bake in a 350°F (180°C) oven for ½ hour or until the tart is set.

Serves 6.

Celery Au Gratin

3 heads of celery
3 tablespoons (45 g) butter
2½ tablespoons plain flour
1¼ cups (300 ml) milk

⅔ cup grated cheese
salt and pepper
¼ cup (65 ml) cream
dried bread crumbs

1. Trim the heads of celery and cut to about 6 inches (15 cm). (The tops can be kept for soup.)
2. Drop the heads into a large saucepan of boiling salted water and cook for 20 minutes or until tender.
3. Melt the butter in a small saucepan and stir in the flour. Cook for one minute, then slowly add the milk, stirring constantly.
4. Add the grated cheese and salt and pepper to taste. Stir until the cheese is melted.
5. Drain the celery and cut the heads in half. Put in a buttered baking dish and pour over the cheese sauce.
6. Spoon on the cream and sprinkle with the bread crumbs.
7. Bake in a 400°F (200°C) oven for 20 minutes.

Serves 6.

Rice with Mushrooms

3 medium onions, chopped
3 tablespoons (45 g) butter
1 lb (500 g) button
   mushrooms
1 cup (250 g) white wine
1 lb (500 g) rice

5 cups (1¼ liters) stock
⅔ cup Parmesan cheese
3 tablespoons (45 g) butter
⅔ cup (165 ml) cream
salt and pepper
chopped chives

1. Saute the onions in the butter until golden brown.
2. Quarter the mushrooms and add to the onions. Stir until the mushrooms are coated with the butter.
3. Add the wine and boil rapidly until wine has evaporated.
4. Stir in the rice and pour on half the stock. Add the stock a little at a time until it is absorbed and the rice is tender.
5. Stir in half the cheese, the butter and the cream. Season to taste with salt and pepper.
6. Serve sprinkled with the remaining cheese and chopped chives.

Serves 6.

Hot Slaw

1 lb (500 g) white cabbage	½ teaspoon salt
½ lb (250 g) red cabbage	2½ tablespoons sugar
⅔ cup (165 ml) vinegar	2½ tablespoons water
4 teaspoons (20 g) butter	2 egg yolks
1 teaspoon dry mustard	⅔ cup (165 g) sour cream

1. Shred the cabbage and soak separately in cold water for ½ hour.
2. Mix together the vinegar, butter, mustard, salt, sugar, water and egg yolks in the top of a double boiler. Place over simmering water and cook, stirring constantly, until the mixture thickens.
3. Stir a little of the mixture into the sour cream. Add the sour cream to the mixture and heat through.
4. Drain the cabbage well and mix together in a large bowl.
5. Pour over the hot sauce, mix thoroughly and serve immediately.

Serves 4-6.

Baked Stuffed Potatoes

6 medium potatoes
⅔ cup (165 ml) milk
1 egg
2 cups grated cheddar
   cheese
4 tablespoons (60 g) butter
salt and cayenne

1. Scrub the potatoes, then bake in a 350°F (180°C) oven for 1½ hours.
2. Cut the potatoes in half lengthwise and gently fork out the flesh taking care not to break the skin. Reserve the skin.
3. Bring the milk to a boil then beat into the potatoes until smooth.
4. Beat in the egg, cheese, butter and salt and cayenne to taste.
5. Spoon the mixture into the potato skin, sprinkle with a little cayenne and bake in a 350°F (180°C) oven for 15 minutes.

Serves 6.

Easy Cauliflower and Cheese

1 large cauliflower
1½ cups (375 ml) cream
1 cup grated Gruyere cheese
salt and pepper

1. Cut the cauliflower into flowerets and cook in boiling salted water for five minutes. Drain.
2. Place the cauliflower in an ovenproof dish.
3. Season the cream with salt and pepper and pour over the cauliflower.
4. Cover with the grated cheese and bake in a 450°F (230°C) oven for 20 minutes.

Serves 6.

Vegetable Pilau

1 cup rice
3 tablespoons (45 g) butter
1 medium onion, sliced
½ teaspoon cumin seeds
4 cardamoms
2 cloves garlic, minced
½ lb (250 g) green beans, sliced

2 medium carrots, diced
1 green pepper, chopped
2 tomatoes, chopped
salt and pepper
¼ cup chopped walnuts

1. Soak the rice in enough cold water to cover for ½ hour. Drain and cook in boiling salted water for ten minutes. Drain well in a colander.
2. Saute the onion in the butter until transparent.
3. Add the cumin seeds, cardamoms and garlic and cook until golden brown.
4. Add the beans and carrots and fry for three minutes.
5. Mix in the green pepper and tomatoes and salt and pepper to taste. Cook for five minutes over a low heat.
6. Stir in the rice and walnuts and serve immediately.

Serves 4-6.

Eggplant with Cheese and Tomatoes

3 lb (1½ kg) eggplant
salt
1½ tablespoons oil
1 medium onion, chopped
1 clove garlic, minced
2 lb (1 kg) tomatoes
1 teaspoon thyme

1 teaspoon oregano
oil for frying
¾ cup Parmesan cheese
1 lb (500 g) Mozarella cheese
4 teaspoons (20 g) butter

1. Slice the eggplant lengthwise and sprinkle with salt. Put slices in a colander with a plate on top and allow to drain for one hour.
2. Saute the onion and garlic in the oil until transparent.
3. Add the peeled and chopped tomatoes, thyme and oregano and cook over a low heat for about ½ hour.
4. Rinse the eggplant slices and dry them thoroughly. Heat some oil and brown them on both sides, cooking only a few at a time. Drain well on absorbent paper.
5. Put a layer of eggplant on a baking dish and cover with a layer of the tomato mixture seasoned well with salt. Sprinkle on some Parmesan cheese. Repeat the layers ending with a layer of tomato sauce.
6. Slice the Mozarella cheese and arrange on the top. Dot with the butter.
7. Bake in a 325°F (160°C) oven for one hour.

Serves 6.

Potato Puffs

⅓ cup instant nonfat dry milk
⅓ cup (85 ml) water
2 cups mashed potatoes
1 medium onion, minced
1 egg, beaten
1 teaspoon salt

⅛ teaspoon cayenne
1 cup dried bread crumbs
½ cup grated Parmesan cheese
4 tablespoons (60 ml) melted butter

1. Beat the instant milk and water until thick and smooth.
2. Add the potatoes, onion, egg, salt and cayenne.
3. Form in small balls.
4. Mix together the bread crumbs, cheese and butter.
5. Roll the potato balls in the crumb mixture and place on a buttered baking sheet.
6. Bake in a 350°F (180°C) oven for ½ hour or until golden brown.

Serves 6.

Spinach Tart

Pastry:
1 cup plain flour
½ teaspoon salt
⅓ cup (85 g) butter
cold water

Filling:
2 lb (1 kg) spinach
2 teaspoons salt
3 tablespoons (45 g)
   butter

2½ tablespoons plain flour
1¼ cups (300 ml) milk
2 cloves garlic, minced
4 tablespoons grated
   cheese
salt
freshly ground black
   pepper

1. Sift the flour and salt and rub in the butter until the mixture resembles fine bread crumbs. Add only enough cold water to form a firm dough. Roll out and line a 9-inch (23-cm) flan case. Prick the pastry and bake in a 400°F (200°C) oven for 15 minutes.
2. Wash the spinach several times in cold water. Add salt, cook in a covered saucepan with no extra water added. Drain for at least 15 minutes.
3. Melt the butter in a small saucepan and add the flour. Cook for 30 seconds, then slowly add the milk, stirring constantly. Cook until thick and smooth. Stir in the garlic and grated cheese.
4. Chop the drained spinach and mix with the white sauce. Season to taste with salt and ground black pepper.
5. Spoon into the flan case and bake in a 400°F (200°C) oven for about 20 minutes.

Serves 4.

Stuffed Zucchini

12 small zucchini
1 medium onion, chopped
3 tablespoons (45 g) butter
2½ oz (75 g) pine nuts
4 tablespoons uncooked rice
1 clove garlic, minced
⅛ teaspoon oregano
1¼ cups (300 ml) boiling
   vegetable stock
salt and pepper

2½ tablespoons oil
Sauce:
2 eggs
2 tablespoons lemon juice
salt and pepper
1 teaspoon grated lemon
   rind
⅔ cup (165 ml) vegetable
   stock

1. Cut the zucchini in half lengthwise. Carefully scoop out the pulp.
2. Saute the onion in the butter until transparent.
3. Add the pine nuts and cook for five minutes.
4. Stir in the rice and cook for another three minutes.
5. Chop the zucchini pulp and add to the mixture with the garlic, oregano and boiling stock. Cover and simmer for about 15 minutes or until the rice is tender. Add more stock if necessary. Season to taste with salt and pepper.
6. Saute the zucchini shells in the oil until just soft.
7. Fill the shells with the pine nut-rice mixture and arrange in a shallow buttered baking dish. Cover with aluminum foil and bake in a 350°F (180°C) oven for 30 minutes.
8. Separate the eggs and beat the egg whites until stiff.
9. Lightly beat egg yolks and add to the whites in the top of a double boiler.
10. Put over simmering water and add the salt and pepper to taste.
11. Alternately add the lemon juice and vegetable stock a few drops at a time, beating constantly. Stir in the lemon rind.
12. Serve the zucchini with the sauce poured over them.

Serves 4-6.

Beans with Spinach

1 cup dried beans
1 teaspoon salt
4 tablespoons oil
4 cloves garlic, minced
2½ tablespoons chopped
  parsley

1½ teaspoons paprika
1 lb (500 g) tomatoes,
  peeled and chopped
1 lb (500 g) spinach
salt

1. Soak the beans in enough water to cover for two hours. Drain and cook in fresh unsalted water to cover until almost cooked. Add the teaspoon of salt and cook until tender. Drain.
2. Heat the oil and saute the garlic until brown.
3. Add the paprika and cook for one minute. Add the garlic and paprika to the beans.
4. In the frypan, cook tomatoes for 20 minutes over medium heat.
5. Add the beans and cook for 20 minutes.
6. Wash the spinach well, put into a saucepan with no extra water and cook, covered, until tender. Drain and chop.
7. Stir the spinach into the bean mixture and cook for 15 minutes, stirring frequently.

Serves 4.

Ratatouille

2 lb (1 kg) tomatoes, peeled
  and chopped
½ cup (125 ml) oil
3 medium onions, thickly
  sliced
3 cloves garlic, minced
2 red peppers, cut in
  squares

1 lb (500 g) zucchini, sliced
1 eggplant, peeled and
  cubed
salt and pepper
pinch of sugar

1. Heat half the oil and simmer the tomatoes for ten minutes.
2. In another frypan heat the remaining oil and saute the onions and garlic for five minutes.
3. Add the pepper, zucchini and eggplant to the onions and cook over a low heat for 15 minutes, stirring frequently.
4. Add the tomatoes, salt and pepper to taste and a pinch of sugar and cook until all the vegetables are tender.

Serves 6.

Italian Stuffed Peppers

4 large peppers, red or
green
½ cup (125 ml) olive oil
1 cup dried bread crumbs
4 tablespoons raisins
12 black olives, pitted and
chopped
2½ tablespoons chopped
parsley

6 anchovy fillets, chopped
1½ tablespoons chopped basil
2½ tablespoons capers
1 teaspoon salt
½ teaspoon pepper
4 tablespoons oil

1. Wash the peppers and cut around the stem, removing it with the seeds.
2. Mix together the olive oil, bread crumbs, raisins, olives, parsley, anchovy fillets, basil, capers, salt and pepper.
3. Stuff the peppers and put into a deep baking dish.
4. Pour one tablespoon oil on top of each pepper and bake in a 375°F (190°C) oven for one hour.

Serves 4.

Mushrooms with Cream Sauce

1½ lb (750 g) mushrooms
4 tablespoons (60 g) butter
1 small onion, chopped
¼ cup (65 ml) sherry

Cream Sauce:
3 tablespoons (45 g) butter
2½ tablespoons plain flour
1 cup (250 ml) milk, warm

1 cup (250 ml) cream,
warm
2 egg yolks
2½ tablespoons water
1 teaspoon salt
¼ teaspoon cayenne
¼ teaspoon nutmeg
toast

1. Wipe the mushrooms with a damp cloth. If large cut them in half or quarter them. Otherwise leave whole.
2. Melt the butter in a large frypan and saute the mushrooms with the onion for ten minutes.
3. Add the sherry and simmer for two minutes.
4. In a small saucepan melt the butter and stir in the flour. Cook for one minute.
5. Mix together the milk and the cream and slowly add to the butter and flour mixture, stirring constantly. Cook until thickened.
6. Beat the egg yolks with the water and add to the sauce, stirring constantly.
7. Stir in the salt, cayenne and nutmeg.
8. Pour onto the mushrooms and mix well.
9. Serve on hot toast.

Serves 4-6.

TABLE OF THE COMPOSITION OF FOODS

. . denotes lack of reliable data for constituent believed to be present.
Zero indicates that the amount of a constituent probably is none or is too small to measure.
Tr indicates that traces of the constituent are known to be present.

g = gramme
kcal = kilocalorie
mg = milligramme
oz = ounce
µg = microgramme (one thousanth of a milligramme)

Foods	Descriptive measure	Weight in ounces	Weight in grammes	Kilo-calories	Protein	Fat	Carbo-hydrate	Cal-cium	Iron	Sodium	Retinol activity	Thia-mine	Ribo-flavin	Niacin	Ascor-bic acid
				kcal	g	g	g	mg	mg	mg	µg	µg	mg	mg	mg
MEAT, POULTRY, FISH, EGGS, NUTS AND PULSES—															
Meats—															
Beef, corned, boiled	3 slices (5 × 2¾ × ⅛)" each	2½	75	**264**	15.8	21.2	0	9	2.2	1,305	. .	15	0.13	1.5	0
hamburger with cereal	1 patty (3¼ × 3¼ × ⅜)"	2⅝	75	**223**	11.4	14.8	11.9	24	1.7	1,821	9	76	0.09	2.3	0
meat sauce	2 tablespoons	1⅞	54	**137**	7.6	11.0	1.6	8	1.3	84	47	41	0.07	1.6	8
roast, lean	1 slice (3 × 3 × ½)"	2½	75	**168**	20.1	9.2	0	5	4.0	53	5	69	0.26	3.2	0
steak, grilled, average	1 rump steak	4½	130	**436**	31.8	33.0	0	22	4.8	121	19	92	0.24	6.3	0
lean	1 rump steak	5	140	**280**	39.6	12.3	0	22	6.0	122	9	109	0.32	8.1	0
casserole with vegetables	¾ cup	6	170	**289**	17.0	19.3	10.0	24	2.8	564	217	43	1.00	2.3	10
casserole without vegetables	¾ cup	6	170	**303**	17.3	20.2	9.6	20	2.8	617	58	41	1.00	2.5	Tr
Chicken, boiled, breast, lean	1 breast No. 7 chicken	4	115	**228**	30.2	9.7	0	16	2.2	113	69	60	0.17	6.9	0
fried, leg	1 leg No. 7 chicken	4½	130	**328**	37.1	17.0	3.7	20	2.7	122	62	89	0.44	11.8	0
roasted	2 slices (3 × 3 × ¼)" each	2½	75	**150**	21.8	7.1	0	12	1.6	60	36	59	0.12	5.9	0
Duck, roasted	2 slices (3½ × 2½ × ¼)" each	2½	75	**235**	17.1	17.7	0	14	4.4	146	. .	60	0.20	4.7	0
Lamb, casserole with vegetables	¾ cup	6	170	**238**	15.3	14.4	13.9	26	1.8	1,013	451	139	0.15	3.5	12
casserole without vegetables	¾ cup	6	170	**249**	15.6	14.4	13.6	20	1.8	1,131	62	148	0.17	3.9	2
chops—															
chump, grilled average	2 chops (5½ × 4½ × ½)" no bone	3¾	110	**390**	20.5	33.8	0	11	2.2	100	. .	120	0.20	4.5	0
lean	2 chops, trimmed, no bone	3¼	95	**273**	20.5	20.8	0	11	2.2	100	. .	120	0.20	4.5	0
loin, grilled, average	2 chops (4 × 2¼ × ⅝)" no bone	4½	130	**473**	24.0	41.3	0	13	2.6	118	. .	142	0.23	5.3	0
lean	2 chops no bone, trimmed	2¾	80	**248**	24.0	16.3	0	13	2.6	118	. .	142	0.23	5.3	0
roast leg	2 slices (3 × 3 × ¼)" each	2½	75	**267**	14.8	23.1	0	5	2.2	53	Tr	90	0.19	3.8	0

MEAT, POULTRY, FISH, EGGS, NUTS AND PULSES—continued

Meats—continued

Foods	Descriptive measure	Weight in ounces	Weight in grammes	Kilocalories kcal	Protein g	Fat g	Carbohydrate g	Calcium mg	Iron mg	Sodium mg	Retinol activity µg	Thiamine µg	Riboflavin mg	Niacin mg	Ascorbic acid mg
Pork, bacon, fried	1 strip 13" long (40 g raw)	¾	21	142	4.1	13.4	0.4	5	0.4	665	0	83	0.05	0.8	0
grilled	1 strip (40 g raw)	½	15	99	4.1	8.9	0.4	4	0.4	499	0	76	0.05	0.8	0
chops, grilled	1 average	2¾	80	348	17.4	30.4	0	9	2.3	92	0	581	0.14	3.6	0
ham, cooked	2 slices (5½ × 3¾ × ⅛)" each	2	60	233	9.7	21.2	0	6	1.4	663	0	375	0.12	2.2	0
sweet and sour pork	½ cup	3¾	110	397	9.3	36.3	9.4	15	1.5	123	101	231	0.08	1.9	10
Rabbit, stewed	¾ cup	6	170	320	45.2	13.0	3.4	32	3.2	88	...	73	0.08	15.3	0
Turkey, roasted	2 slices (3 × 3 × ¼)" each	2½	75	206	22.0	12.3	0	26	3.8	60	...	60	0.12	7.4	0
Veal, cutlet, crumbed and fried	2 average no bone	5	140	400	27.7	25.6	12.1	27	4.3	295	...	147	0.32	8.5	0
fried	2 average no bone	4⅛	120	355	32.1	24.0	0	18	4.8	151	...	151	0.36	9.7	0
grilled	2 average no bone	3½	100	247	30.7	13.0	0	17	4.6	144	—	145	0.32	9.2	—

Offal—

Foods	Descriptive measure	Weight in ounces	Weight in grammes	Kilocalories kcal	Protein g	Fat g	Carbohydrate g	Calcium mg	Iron mg	Sodium mg	Retinol activity µg	Thiamine µg	Riboflavin mg	Niacin mg	Ascorbic acid mg
Brains, crumbed and fried	1 set	5	140	407	16.2	29.5	15.5	60	4.3	534	0	196	0.25	5.0	18
Kidney, sheep, grilled	1 kidney	1¼	35	75	9.3	3.9	Tr	5	4.9	88	117	135	1.06	3.2	3
Liver, floured, fried	1 slice (5 × 2 ×½)"	2	60	158	18.5	6.2	8.2	6	8.3	71	6,396	159	2.23	9.2	16
Tripe, cooked with parsley sauce	¾ cup	6	170	170	16.6	6.4	10.3	86	0.3	2,573	68	37	0.25	1.5	2

Sausage meats—

Foods	Descriptive measure	Weight in ounces	Weight in grammes	Kilocalories kcal	Protein g	Fat g	Carbohydrate g	Calcium mg	Iron mg	Sodium mg	Retinol activity µg	Thiamine µg	Riboflavin mg	Niacin mg	Ascorbic acid mg
Devon/Bologna	2 slices (4 × 4 × ⅛)" each	1¾	50	120	7.3	9.2	1.9	5	1.1	650	...	90	0.10	1.4	0
Frankfurters, boiled	2 average (1¼ × 1¼ × 3)" each	3½	100	280	13.0	23.8	2.0	6	1.3	1,084	...	160	0.18	2.5	0
Liverwurst	2 slices (3" diam. ¼" thick)	2	60	166	9.8	13.3	1.0	5	3.2		958	108	0.70	2.9	0
Salami	2 slices (3 × 3 ×¼") each	2	60	241	13.3	20.4	Tr	7	2.0			139	0.03	0.6	0
Sausage, beef, grilled, thick	2 (1¼ × 1¼ × 3½)" each	3¾	110	339	16.7	24.3	10.5	14	3.0			83	0.14	3.4	0
thin	2 (6 × ¾ × 4½)" each	2½	75	231	11.4	16.6	7.2	10	2.1			56	0.10	2.3	0
pork, grilled, thick	2 (1¼ × 1¼ × 3½)" each	3¾	110	335	15.9	25.4	15.4	22	2.6	1,317	0	470	0.18	2.5	0
thin	2 (6 × ¾ c 4½)" each	2½	75	242	10.9	17.3	10.5	15	1.8	899	0	321	0.13	1.9	0

Fish—

Foods	Descriptive measure	Weight in ounces	Weight in grammes	Kilocalories kcal	Protein g	Fat g	Carbohydrate g	Calcium mg	Iron mg	Sodium mg	Retinol activity µg	Thiamine µg	Riboflavin mg	Niacin mg	Ascorbic acid mg
Crab, meat, canned	½ cup flakes	3⅛	90	90	15.5	2.2	1.0	41	0.7	900	...	72	0.07	1.7	...
Fish, baked	1 fillet (4 × 2½ × ½)"	2	60	78	13.4	2.3	0	26	0.5	85	...	45	0.07	2.3	...
crumbed and fried	1 fillet (4 × 2½ × ½)"	3½	100	253	18.4	14.4	11.6	253	1.4	187	24	60	0.11	2.0	...

MEAT, POULTRY, FISH, EGGS, NUTS AND PULSES—continued

Foods	Descriptive measure	Weight in ounces	Weight in grammes	Kilocalories kcal	Protein g	Fat g	Carbohydrate g	Calcium mg	Iron mg	Sodium mg	Retinol activity µg	Thiamine µg	Riboflavin mg	Niacin mg	Ascorbic acid mg
Fish—continued															
fried in batter	1 fillet (4 × 2½ × ½)"	3½	100	249	19.2	13.1	14.3	249	1.3	113	85	80	0.14	1.6	..
steamed	1 fillet (4 × 2½ × ½)"	2½	75	78	13.4	2.3	0	26	0.5	85	..	45	0.07	2.3	..
Herring, canned	2 small	3½	100	201	19.3	13.1	0	147	1.8	..	29	20	0.18	3.4	0
Lobster, canned	½ cup meat	3⅛	90	86	16.8	1.3	0.3	56	0.7	189	..	90	0.06	5.7	..
Mackerel, canned	1 piece (4½ × 2 × ¾)"	3½	100	182	19.2	11.1	0	183	2.0	..	108	59	0.20	2.8	0
Oysters, fresh	1 dozen medium	4¼	120	82	10.4	1.8	4.9	106	6.8	88	105	180	0.23	2.4	..
Prawns, fried in batter	2 to 3 medium	3⅛	90	203	18.2	9.7	9.0	65	1.8	167	..	36	0.07	1.4	..
canned	½ cup	3⅛	90	109	21.7	1.4	0.6	104	1.8	..	9	54	0.03	8.5	..
Salmon, canned	½ cup	4⅛	120	196	25.8	9.3	0	221	1.3	636	86	39	0.16	4.0	0
smoked	3 small pieces	1¾	50	83	10.8	4.7	0	9	0.3	..	64	50	0.14	3.3	0
Sardines, canned in oil	4 to 5 small	2	60	171	12.5	13.4	..	215	2.2	351	34	18	0.18	3.3	0
Tuna, canned in water	½ (6½ oz tin)	3⅛	90	114	25.2	0.8	..	14	1.4	788	..	..	0.09	11.9	..
Eggs—															
Egg, whole, raw	1 large	1¾	50	80	6.3	5.8	0.4	27	1.2	61	141	51	0.15	0.05	0
	1 medium	1½	45	72	5.6	5.2	0.3	24	1.1	54	128	50	0.14	0.04	0
	1 small	1⅜	39	62	4.9	4.5	0.3	21	1.0	48	110	40	0.12	0.04	0
white, raw	1 medium	1	28	14	2.9	Tr	0.2	2	Tr	44	0	6	0.08	0.03	0
yolk, raw	1 medium	⅝	17	59	2.8	5.2	0.1	22	1.1	10	128	44	0.07	0.01	0
boiled	1 medium	1½	45	72	5.6	5.2	0.3	24	1.1	54	128	39	0.13	0.04	0
fried	1 medium	1⅝	48	108	5.6	9.3	0.3	25	1.1	96	184	40	0.13	0.04	0
omelette, plain	2 medium	3½	100	248	11.4	22.6	0.8	52	2.2	1,036	426	86	0.26	0.08	0
poached	1 medium	1½	45	72	5.6	5.2	0.3	24	1.1	54	128	40	0.12	0.03	0
scrambled with milk and butter	1 medium	2⅜	70	148	6.6	12.4	1.8	63	1.1	534	226	55	0.18	0.07	Tr
Nuts and Pulses—															
Almonds, roasted and salted	26 no.	1	30	188	5.8	17.0	5.6	74	1.2	60	0	72	0.22	1.0	0

Foods	Descriptive measure	Weight in ounces	Weight in grammes	Kilo-calories kcal	Protein g	Fat g	Carbo-hydrate g	Cal-cium mg	Iron mg	Sodium mg	Retinol activity µg	Thia-mine µg	Ribo-flavin mg	Niacin mg	Ascor-bic acid mg
MEAT, POULTRY, FISH, EGGS, NUTS AND PULSES—*continued*															
Nuts and Pulses—*continued*															
Cashewnuts, roasted	15 no.	1	30	**172**	5.4	14.2	8.4	12	1.4	4	0	168	0.06	0.6	0
Coconut, freshmeat	2 pieces (1× 1 × ⅜)" each	1	30	**110**	1.0	10.6	4.6	4	0.6	6	0	16	Tr	0.2	Tr
shredded, dry	¼ cup	½	15	**101**	1.0	9.4	4.4	3	0.5	2	0	6	Tr	0.1	0
Peanuts, roasted and salted	36 to 38 no.	1	30	**174**	7.8	14.6	5.8	22	0.8	132	0	86	0.06	5.0	0
Peanut butter	1 tablespoon	¾	21	**119**	5.5	9.7	3.4	14	0.5	160	..	6	0.09	4.2	..
Peas, split, boiled	⅓ cup	2	56	**64**	4.5	0.2	11.6	8	1.0	7	4	98	0.05	0.5	0
Walnuts, shelled	15 halves	1	30	**192**	4.4	19.0	4.5	25	0.7	..	0	117	0.04	0.3	Tr
MILK AND MILK PRODUCTS—															
Butter and cream—refer to fat group															
Cheese—															
Cottage, creamed	1 tablespoon	⅝	20	**21**	2.7	0.8	0.6	19	Tr	45	10	6	0.05	Tr	0
Cream cheese	1 tablespoon	⅝	19	**66**	1.7	6.1	0.6	8	Tr	64	78	4	0.04	Tr	0
Grating cheese—															
Parmesan cheese	1 tablespoon	⅜	9	**41**	3.7	2.9	.0	109	Tr	159	38	2	0.07	Tr	0
Natural cheddar	1 piece (1 × 1 × 1)"	⅝	20	**80**	5.2	6.6	0	172	0.2	122	84	7	0.09	Tr	0
Processed cheddar	1 slice (3¾ × 3½ × ⅛)"	¾	21	**67**	4.6	5.3	0.2	132	0.2	205	67	4	0.10	Tr	0
Processed spread, cheddar	1 tablespoon	⅝	19	**63**	4.0	5.1	0.2	122	0.1	207	66	..	..	..	0
Milk—															
Condensed, sweetened	1 tablespoon	⅞	27	**93**	2.5	2.5	14.7	87	Tr	40	23	25	0.10	Tr	Tr
unsweetened	1 tablespoon	¾	21	**32**	1.7	1.7	2.2	62	Tr	38	17	17	0.08	Tr	Tr
Dessert, blancmange	½ cup	4⅜	125	**138**	4.0	4.5	20.0	143	0.3	59	43	54	0.20	0.3	Tr
custard, baked with egg	½ cup	4½	130	**142**	6.8	6.8	12.9	146	0.7	87	98	61	0.23	0.1	Tr
custard sauce with powder	¼ cup	2⅜	70	**65**	2.4	2.4	8.0	81	0.1	34	28	28	0.11	0.1	Tr
ice-cream, homemade	2 ice-cream scoops (4 of 2" diam.)	2	60	**98**	4.3	4.3	9.9	145	0.1	89	41	39	0.18	0.1	1
plain and flavoured	2 ice-cream scoops	2¼	64	**129**	3.4	7.1	13.2	90	0.1	50	74	30	0.13	0.1	1
junket	1 serve	3½	100	**79**	3.1	3.3	9.0	106	0.1	..	..	33	0.15	0.1	..

Foods	Descriptive measure	Weight in ounces	Weight in grammes	Kilocalories kcal	Protein g	Fat g	Carbohydrate g	Calcium mg	Iron mg	Sodium mg	Retinol activity µg	Thiamine µg	Riboflavin mg	Niacin mg	Ascorbic acid mg
MILK AND MILK PRODUCTS— continued															
Fluid, cow buttermilk, cultured															
flavoured	½ cup	4	115	44	4.0	0.9	4.8	132	0.1	64	Tr	44	0.20	0.1	1
	1 carton	10	285	245	10.0	10.0	29.6	314	0.6	125	88	100	0.46	0.3	3
skimmed	1 cup	8	235	82	8.0	0.2	11.3	289	0.2	120	.	96	0.42	0.2	2
whole	1 cup	8	230	154	7.6	8.7	10.5	264	0.2	128	94	85	0.39	0.2	2
Powder, full cream	1 tablespoon	3/8	9	46	2.6	2.4	3.3	87	Tr	40	24	25	0.10	0.1	Tr
malted	1 tablespoon	3/8	12	50	1.6	1.0	8.6	34	0.3	57	29	82	0.06	Tr	.
skimmed	1 tablespoon	3/8	11	41	4.2	0.1	5.5	144	0.1	63	1	39	0.22	0.1	.
Yogurt—															
Flavoured and fruit	1 carton	8	235	235	10.1	8.2	25.6	305	Tr	94	88	103	0.44	0.2	2
Plain	1 carton	8	230	165	10.1	8.2	13.1	338	Tr	92	95	115	0.46	0.2	2
Skimmed	1 carton	8	230	119	13.5	0.2	15.8	332	Tr	92	0	105	0.46	0.2	2
FRUIT AND VEGETABLES—															
Fruits—															
Apple, raw, whole	1 small 2½ diameter	3½	100	53	0.3	0.3	13.8	6	0.3	2	7	36	0.03	0.2	6
Apple, stewed, with added sugar	1 small	4	115	94	0.3	0.3	24.4	8	0.3	2	6	32	0.03	0.2	5
canned sweetened	7 pieces with syrup	3½	100	76	0.2	0.1	20.6	4	0.4		3	20	0.01	Tr	4
sauce	1 baby can	4½	127	98	0.2	0.3	23.5	5	0.5	5	3	15	0.03	Tr	29
Apricot, raw, whole	3 medium	3½	100	45	0.8	0.2	11.4	16	0.5	2	245	34	0.05	0.8	8
canned, sweetened	4 medium halves	4½	120	86	0.7	0.1	23.4	12	0.5	1	181	23	0.02	0.3	6
dried, raw	5 halves	⅞	25	66	1.1	0.1	17.1	21	1.1	6	220	2	0.04	0.8	2
Banana, ripe	1 medium 6" long, peeled	3½	100	87	1.1	0.3	22.5	.9	0.6	1	33	62	0.05	0.7	11
Cherries, raw	20 to 22 medium	3½	100	61	0.9	0.4	15.1	18	0.4	2	27	50	0.06	0.4	8
Dates, dried	5 to 6 pitted	1⅛	33	95	0.7	0.2	25.3	22	0.7	1	3	28	0.03	0.7	0
Grapefruit, raw	½ (4" diameter)	4¼	120	44	0.6	0.2	11.0	24	0.3	1	4	53	0.02	0.2	48
Grapes, raw	20 to 22 no.	3½	100	66	0.7	0.4	16.8	18	0.5	2	8	54	0.04	0.2	4

FRUIT AND VEGETABLES—continued

Foods	Descriptive measure	Weight in ounces	Weight in grammes	Kilo- calories kcal	Protein g	Fat g	Carbo- hydrate g	Cal- cium mg	Iron mg	Sodium mg	Retinol activity µg	Thia- mine µg	Ribo- flavin mg	Niacin mg	Ascor- bic acid mg
Fruits—continued															
Lemon, raw	2 slices, 1/8" thickness	1/2	15	5	0.1	Tr	1.5	8	0.1	0	Tr	8	Tr	Tr	7
Mandarine, raw	1 large or 2 small	3 1/2	100	46	0.8	0.3	11.2	37	0.4	2	46	68	0.03	0.2	31
Mango, ripe	1 small (3" diameter)	3 1/2	100	66	0.7	0.2	17.2	10	0.3	7	801	55	0.06	0.9	41
Orange	1 medium (2 3/4" diameter)	4 1/2	130	59	1.2	0.3	14.4	51	0.5	2	30	109	0.04	0.3	65
Passionfruit, raw	1 medium	1	30	27	0.7	0.2	6.3	4	0.4	8	Tr	0	0.03	0.4	7
Pawpaw, raw	1/4 medium (5 × 4)"	3 1/2	100	41	0.6	0.1	10.5	21	0.3	3	131	36	0.04	0.3	64
Peaches, raw, yellow	1 medium	3 7/8	110	45	0.7	0.1	11.7	8	0.6	2	113*	22	0.05	1.1	8
canned, sweetened	5 pieces with syrup	4 1/4	120	82	0.4	0.1	22.0	5	0.4	3	52	12	0.02	0.7	5
Pear, raw	1 medium (3 × 2 1/2)"	5 1/4	150	84	0.6	0.4	21.7	12	0.4	3	3	33	0.06	0.2	8
canned, sweetened	2 halves in syrup	4 1/4	120	77	0.2	0.1	20.8	8	0.2	3	2	12	0.02	0.2	8
Pineapple, raw	1 slice (3 1/2 × 3 1/2 × 3/4)"	2 3/4	80	42	0.4	0.2	10.8	14	0.3	2	36	66	0.03	0.2	21
canned, sweetened	2 slices (2 3/4 × 2 3/4 × 1/2)"	3	90	66	0.4	0.1	17.7	17	0.5	1	7	61	0.02	0.2	8
Strawberries, raw	12 to 14 medium	3 1/2	100	37	0.7	0.5	8.6	24	0.8	2	8	26	0.06	0.4	58
Sultanas, raisins and currants, dried	1 tablespoon	1/2	13	35	0.2	Tr	9.2	9	0.2	5	1	17	0.01	0.1	Tr
Watermelon, raw	1/2 cup balls	3 7/8	110	30	0.5	0.2	7.1	7	0.3	1	65	46	0.04	0.2	6
Fruit salad—															
Fresh fruit	1/2 cup	3 7/8	110	69	0.9	0.3	17.6	17	0.6	4	30	68	0.04	0.4	23
Semi fresh	1/2 cup	3 7/8	110	73	0.5	0.2	19.3	10	0.3	2	25	28	0.03	0.4	10
Tropical canned	1/2 cup	3 7/8	110	79	0.3	0.1	20.9	9	0.3	1	51	15	0.03	0.4	2
Juices—															
Grapefruit, fresh	1/2 cup	4 1/4	120	44	0.6	0.1	11.4	11	0.3	1	0	46	0.02	0.2	47
canned	1/2 cup	4 1/4	120	57	0.6	0.1	15.3	10	0.3	1	0	36	0.02	0.2	36
Orange, fresh	1/2 cup	4 1/4	120	52	0.9	0.3	12.7	38	0.3	2	36	100	0.03	0.3	59
canned	1/2 cup	4 1/4	120	57	0.8	0.2	14.6	12	0.4	1	26	84	0.02	0.3	48
Pineapple, canned	1/2 cup	4 1/4	120	59	0.5	0.1	15.8	16	0.6	1	9	60	0.02	0.2	11
Vegetables—															
Asparagus, canned	3 medium spears	2	60	11	1.0	0.2	1.8	12	0.6	177	31	42	0.05	0.5	9
Beans, baked beans	1/4 cup	2	60	66	3.6	0.3	13.1	25	1.0	..	5	30	0.02	0.3	1

* Retinol activity for white flesh kinds is about 5 µg per 100 g edible raw peach.

Foods	Descriptive measure	Weight in ounces	Weight in grammes	Kilo-calories	Protein	Fat	Carbo-hydrate	Cal-cium	Iron	Sodium	Retinol activity	Thia-mine	Ribo-flavin	Niacin	Ascor-bic acid
				kcal	g	g	g	mg	mg	mg	µg	µg	mg	mg	mg
FRUIT AND VEGETABLES—*continued*															
Beans—*continued*															
french, boiled	½ cup	2	60	**19**	1.0	0.1	4.0	29	0.4	3	38	35	0.04	0.2	7
Beetroot/beets, canned	2 slices	1	30	**10**	0.3	Tr	2.3	4	0.2	71	Tr	3	0.01	Tr	1
Cabbage, raw shredded	⅓ cup	1¼	35	**9**	0.5	0.1	1.9	16	0.2	7	5	20	0.01	0.1	20
Carrots, raw	1 small 4" long	2	60	**22**	0.5	0.1	5.1	24	0.4	39	765	36	0.03	0.3	3
boiled	⅓ cup diced	1¾	50	**15**	0.4	0.1	3.5	18	0.3	23	583	25	0.03	0.2	2
Cauliflower, boiled	½ cup flower pieces	2	60	**14**	1.3	0.1	2.5	12	0.4	6	3	49	0.05	0.3	31
Celery, raw	3 pieces, 2" long	1	30	**6**	0.3	Tr	1.3	14	0.1	40	8	11	0.01	0.1	2
Corn, canned, sweet	¼ cup	1⅜	40	**33**	0.9	0.3	7.3	2	0.3	94	16	48	0.02	0.4	2
canned, cream style	¼ cup	2	60	**49**	1.2	0.4	12.0	2	0.4	141	9	18	0.03	0.6	3
Lettuce, raw	2 small leaves	¾	20	**4**	0.3	Tr	0.6	6	0.1	2	60	11	0.02	Tr	3
Mushrooms, sauteed in butter	6 to 7 small	2	60	**66**	1.4	6.3	2.4	7	0.5	50	43	48	0.24	2.5	Tr
Peas, green, boiled	⅓ cup	2	56	**39**	3.0	0.2	7.6	11	1.0	Tr	39	140	0.08	1.1	11
Potato, baked	1 medium 2¼" diameter	3⅛	90	**164**	2.0	9.1	19.7	10	0.7	6	5	85	0.05	1.1	11
boiled	1 medium	3⅛	90	**72**	1.8	0.1	17.1	8	0.6	5	1	92	0.04	1.0	10
fried (salt added)	17 to 18 pieces (2 × ½ × ½)"	3⅛	90	**241**	3.4	12.7	29.3	13	0.9	200	6	90	0.05	1.5	10
mashed, milk added	⅓ cup	2⅜	70	**44**	1.4	0.5	9.2	16	0.3	210	3	59	0.04	0.6	6
Pumpkin, boiled	¼ cup mashed	2	60	**19**	0.6	0.1	4.2	15	0.3	1	326	21	0.04	0.3	3
Spinach and **silverbeet,** boiled	⅓ cup	2	60	**16**	1.7	0.2	2.7	65	1.8	237	615	48	0.10	0.3	15
Sweet potato, baked	½ small (2 × 2 × 5)"	2	60	**135**	0.8	6.3	19.5	17	0.4	7	0	36	0.03	0.3	12
Tomato, raw	1 medium	3⅞	110	**23**	1.1	0.3	4.5	15	0.5	4	131	66	0.04	0.6	24
Vegetables, mixed, boiled	½ cup	3½	100	**64**	3.2	0.3	13.4	25	1.3	53	498	120	0.07	1.1	8
CEREALS AND CEREAL PRODUCTS—															
Biscuits—															
Cracker, low fat	3 biscuits	⅜	12	**48**	1.3	0.9	8.8	..	..	96	..	..	..	..	..

Foods	Descriptive measure	Weight in ounces	Weight in grammes	Kilo-calories	Protein	Fat	Carbo-hydrate	Cal-cium	Iron	Sodium	Retinol activity	Thia-mine	Ribo-flavin	Niacin	Ascor-bic acid
				kcal	g	g	g	mg	mg	mg	µg	µg	mg	mg	mg
CEREALS AND CEREAL PRODUCTS—*continued*															
Biscuits—*continued*															
Cracker, medium fat	2 biscuits	⅝	18	**85**	1.4	3.3	12.5	..	..	140	..	..	..	..	..
high fat e.g. cheese crackers	3 biscuits	⅜	12	**59**	1.0	3.1	7.1	..	..	110	..	..	..	..	..
Crispbread, rye	2 biscuits	⅝	19	**68**	1.9	0.5	15.0	..	..	99	..	..	..	..	..
wheat	2 biscuits	⅜	11	**46**	1.0	1.2	8.3	5	0.4	55	..	22	..	..	..
Sweet, cream, filled, assorted	1 biscuit	⅝	19	**95**	0.9	4.8	12.8	..	..	..	..	..	..	..	..
plain sweet	2 biscuits	⅝	16	**68**	1.0	2.0	12.3	7	0.2	26	..	8	Tr	0.1	0
shredded wheatmeal	2 biscuits	⅝	16	**69**	1.2	1.9	12.4	7	0.4	75	..	29	0.02	0.2	0
Bread—															
Brown	2 slices (4 × 3½ × ⅓)" each	1¾	50	**121**	4.0	0.9	24.6	10	0.9	269	0	105	0.06	1.2	0
Rye, light	2 slices (4 × 2¾ × ⅓)" each	1½	44	**105**	3.3	0.7	21.6	33	0.7	245	0	76	0.03	0.6	0
White	2 slices (4 × 4 × ⅓)" each	1⅝	46	**112**	3.6	0.7	23.0	6	0.5	233	0	59	0.04	0.4	0
White roll, round	3" diameter	1¾	50	**122**	3.9	0.8	25.0	7	0.5	254	0	64	0.04	0.4	0
White roll, long	7" long	2¼	66	**160**	5.2	1.0	33.2	9	0.7	334	0	85	0.04	0.6	0
White + 4% skim milk powder	2 slices (4 × 4 × ⅓)" each	1⅝	48	**118**	4.0	1.2	23.2	25	0.5	243	0	64	0.05	0.5	0
White, starch reduced	2 slices (3½ × 3½ × ⅓)" each	1¼	36	**88**	3.4	0.9	17.0	5	0.4	..	0	46	0.03	0.3	0
Wholemeal	2 slices (4½ × 4 × ⅓)"	2¼	64	**147**	5.2	1.5	29.9	22	1.9	339	0	175	0.06	1.7	..
Breadcrumbs	2 tablespoons	¾	20	**76**	2.0	0.9	15.0	25	0.6	149	0	46	0.05	0.6	0
Breakfast cereal—															
Branflakes, cornflakes and rice bubbles	1 cup or packet portion	1	28	**104**	2.4	0.2	23.6	9	2.4	270	Tr	454	0.66	4.47	..
Oatmeal, cooked (1:3) (salt added)	1 cup	8	234	**129**	4.7	2.6	23.4	19	1.4	510	..	183	0.05	0.2	0
Wheatflake biscuits	2 biscuits	1⅛	33	**120**	4.2	0.4	24.4	18	1.6	123	..	162	0.04	1.2	..
Flour—															
White, and self raising	1 tablespoon	⅜	10	**36**	1.1	0.2	7.5	5	0.1	73*	0	22	Tr	0.1	0
Grains and starches—															
Macaroni, boiled	1 cup	5¼	150	**171**	4.9	0.8	34.8	12	0.6	..	0	45	0.02	0.6	0
Noodles, boiled	1 cup	5¼	150	**180**	6.1	2.0	34.8	12	0.9	3	23	60	0.03	0.6	0
Rice, boiled salt added	1 cup	5½	160	**171**	3.2	0.3	39.0	11	0.3	598	0	40	0.02	0.6	0

* Value shown is for self-raising flour. Amount of sodium in plain flour is negligible.

Foods	Descriptive measure	Weight in ounces	Weight in grammes	Kilo-calories kcal	Protein g	Fat g	Carbo-hydrate g	Cal-cium mg	Iron mg	Sodium mg	Retinol activity µg	Thia-mine µg	Ribo-flavin mg	Niacin mg	Ascor-bic acid / Alcohol† mg
FATS AND OILS—															
Butter, salted	1 tablespoon	⅔	19	**138**	0.1	15.4	0.1	3	Tr	160	191	3	Tr	Tr	0
Cream, fresh	1 tablespoon	¾	20	**73**	0.4	7.6	0.6	16	Tr	7	100	5	0.02	Tr	Tr
Margarine, table	1 tablespoon	⅔	19	**138**	0.1	15.4	0.1	4	Tr	7	100	5	0.02	Tr	Tr
Oil, salad and cooking	1 tablespoon	⅔	19	**168**	..	18.9	..	..	..	..	..	..	..	..	..
Peanut butter	1 tablespoon	¾	21	**119**	5.5	9.7	3.4	14	0.5	160	..	6	0.09	4.2	..
Salad dressings—															
French dressing, commercial	1 tablespoon	¾	20	**81**	0.1	7.4	3.7	2	0.1	274	..	..	..	..	..
Mayonnaise	1 tablespoon	⅔	19	**135**	0.2	15.0	0.5	3	0.1	113	5	4	Tr	Tr	0
MISCELLANEOUS—															
Beverages—Alcoholic—															Alcohol†
Beer	1 large glass	8	240	**96**	0.7	0	6.9	8	Tr	43	..	6	0.33	0.3	9
Gin, rum, whisky	1 nip	1	30	**69**	0	0	..	..	..	..	..	..	..	..	10
Champagne	1 champagne glass	5	150	**125**	0.3	0	2.9	5	0.8	6	..	..	..	..	18
Liqueurs	1 liqueur glass	¾	20	**68**	0	0	6.3	..	..	..	..	..	..	..	7
Sherry, semi-sweet	1 sherry glass	2	60	**76**	0.2	0	2.6	4	0.2	7	..	..	..	..	9
Wine, red, claret	1 wine glass	3½	100	**86**	0.3	0	0.1	15	0.2	7	..	..	..	..	13
white, sauterne	1 wine glass	3½	100	**89**	0.2	0	4.0	15	0.2	15	..	..	..	..	11
Beverages—non alcoholic—															Ascor-bic acid
Carbonated, average	½ small bottle	6	170	**77**	0	0	20.4	0	0	0	0	0	0	0	..
Chocolate, malted milk shake	1 regular-10 oz. milk	12½	345	**325**	12.1	13.4	38.1	389	0.9	242	133	269	..	..	3
Chocolate milk shake	1 regular-10 oz milk	12	335	**287**	10.9	12.6	31.6	359	0.9	188	133	124	0.92	0.4	3
Thick milk shake, flavoured (not chocolate)	1 regular-10 oz milk	12	345	**293**	11.6	15.0	27.4	390	0.3	193	161	126	0.57	0.3	3
Cordials, syrup, diluted (1:4)	1 glass	8	230	**65**	Tr	..	17.0	4	..	..	..	..	Tr	..	3
Fruit juices—refer to fruit and vegetable group—															

† Alcoholic beverages do not contain any ascorbic acid.

Foods	Descriptive measure	Weight in ounces	Weight in grammes	Kilo-calories kcal	Protein g	Fat g	Carbo-hydrate g	Cal-cium mg	Iron mg	Sodium mg	Retinol activity µg	Thia-mine µg	Ribo-flavin mg	Niacin mg	Ascor-bic acid mg
MISCELLANEOUS—*continued*															
Beverages—*continued*															
Gingerale	1 glass	8	230	**78**	..	..	20.4	0	0	16	0	0	0	0	0
Ovaltine (no sugar added)—															
made in water	1 glass water and 2 tbsp. Ovaltine	8	240	**54**	2.0	0.8	9.8	38	2.6	24	48	246	0.16	3.2	6
made in milk	1 glass	8	230	**177**	8.7	8.9	17.4	282	2.0	145	140	271	0.50	2.3	7
Cakes, puddings, etc.—															
Bun, sweet, plain	1 average	1¾	50	**158**	3.1	4.8	25.6	27	0.9	..	21	85	0.09	0.8	0
iced	1 average	2	58	**189**	3.1	4.8	33.6	27	0.9	..	21	85	0.09	0.8	0
hot cross	1 average	1¼	35	**120**	2.6	3.2	20.0	19	0.6	..	14	82	0.08	0.6	0
Cheese cake	⅙ of 8" cake	4	120	**341**	10.2	21.1	27.9	85	0.6	248	250	41	0.19	0.1	Tr
Doughnut, cake type	1 average	1⅜	40	**141**	2.6	7.0	20.0	14	0.5	183	92	48	0.04	0.2	Tr
Fruit cake, light	1 slice (3 × 2 × ½)"	1⅛	33	**128**	2.0	6.0	18.1	16	0.4	58	69	37	0.03	0.2	Tr
Jelly, gelatin	1 serve	3½	100	**97**	2.9	0	21.8	..	..	..	..	..	..	..	..
Jelly, low calorie (Jell Quick)	1 serve	3½	100	**4**	..	..	..	18	0.3	192	..	..	..	..	..
Lamingtons	1 piece (2½ × 1½ × 1½)"	2	60	**214**	3.8	7.8	33.5	20	1.2	86	40	40	0.06	0.1	Tr
Milkpuddings—refer to milk group															
Pie, fruit	⅙ of 8" pie	5	140	**330**	3.3	12.4	52.6	8	0.4	403	..	28	0.22	0.4	Tr
Scones/biscuits, plain	1 scone (2 × 2 × 2)"	1	30	**106**	2.9	3.3	16.3	41	0.3	186	46	52	0.04	0.3	0
Sponge cake, plain	⅛ of 7" cake 2" high	1	30	**94**	2.8	1.8	16.5	17	0.5	51	41	35	0.05	0.1	..
fresh cream filled & iced	⅛ of 7" cake	1¾	50	**152**	2.9	5.2	23.7	23	0.5	59	84	37	0.06	0.2	..
mock cream filled & ice	⅛ of 7" cake	1¾	50	**135**	2.7	2.4	26.3	24	0.5	48	45	34	0.06	0.2	..
Tea cake, plain	1 slice (3× 2 × ½)"	1¼	35	**124**	2.8	3.4	19.7	38	0.4	211	44	42	0.04	0.1	0
Confectionary—															
Boiled sweets	1 average piece	⅓	8	**28**	Tr	Tr	7.3	Tr	Tr	2	..	..	..	..	0
Butterscotch	1 average piece	⅙	5	**21**	Tr	0.4	4.5	1	0	3	4	0	0	0	0
Candied fruits (apricot, fig, pineapple)	1 large fruit or 1 ring pineapple	1¼	35	**104**	1.2	Tr	25.6	23	0.2	..	7*	23	0.02	0.1	0
Caramel	1 cube ¾"	⅓	8	**34**	Tr	0.9	6.5	12	1.4	16	..	..	..	..	0

Foods	Descriptive measure	Weight in ounces	Weight in grammes	Kilo-calories	Protein	Fat	Carbo-hydrate	Cal-cium	Iron	Sodium	Retinol activity	Thia-mine	Ribo-flavin	Niacin	Ascor-bic acid
				kcal	g	g	g	mg	mg	mg	µg	µg	mg	mg	mg
MISCELLANEOUS—*continued*															
Confectionary—*continued*															
Chocolate, block milk	4 to 6 small squares	⅔	20	**108**	1.8	6.2	11.2	59	0.4	25	10	24	0.08	0.1	0
nut milk	4 to 6 small squares	⅔	20	**109**	2.8	7.6	8.9	35	0.3	13	..	50	0.05	1.0	0
plain dark	4 to 6 small squares	⅔	20	**116**	0.8	6.0	12.5	7	..	3	4	18	0.03	0.1	0
Ice-cream—refer to milk group															
Life-saver type	1 packet of 10 pieces	½	13	**60**	Tr	..	16.5	..	..	..	..	..	..	..	..
Liquorice, all sorts	2 average	½	15	**48**	0.3	Tr	12.1	2	0.2	6	0	0	0	0	0
plain	6 × 1" pieces	1	28	**97**	1.3	1.5	19.4	..	..	..	..	..	..	..	..
Marshmallow	2 average pieces	⅓	9	**29**	0.2	Tr	7.3	2	0.1	0	0	0	0	0	0
Peanut brittle	1 piece (2½ × 2½ × ½)"	1	30	**129**	2.1	3.9	22.8	11	0.6	9	Tr	36	0.01	1.2	0
Popcorn plain	1 cup	½	15	**57**	0.9	0.5	12.8	1	0.2	Tr	..	..	0.01	0.1	0
Snacks—															
Hamburger	Standard breadroll, hamburger and onion	5	145	**355**	15.3	13.2	43.6	22	2.2	1,591	10	143	0.14	2.3	0
Hotdog	Breadroll and 1 frankfurt	4	115	**321**	13.0	16.6	29.6	11	1.5	1,002	..	179	0.15	2.2	0
Meat pie	4½" diameter	5¾	163	**518**	13.4	32.0	44.9	58	2.1	494	327	174	2.30	2.4	0
Olives, pickled	4 or 5 no	⅔	20	**40**	0.3	3.4	0.4	18	0.3	180	5	..	..	..	..
Sandwiches, white bread	2 slices and butter	2¼	60	**207**	4.4	8.6	28.3	8	0.6	367	190	76	0.04	0.5	0
plus baked beans	1 tablespoon	¾	20	**22**	1.2	0.1	4.4	8	0.3	..	2	10	0.01	0.1	..
plus cheese	1 slice (packet)	¾	21	**67**	4.6	5.3	0.2	132	0.2	205	67	4	0.10	Tr	0
plus egg	½ egg	¾	22	**36**	2.8	2.6	0.1	12	0.6	27	62	20	0.06	Tr	0
plus ham	1 slice (3½ × 3½ × ⅛)"	¾	22	**145**	13.7	9.2	Tr	8	2.0	825	..	398	0.14	2.9	0
plus meat	1 slice (3 × 3 × ⅙)"	¾	25	**50**	7.3	2.4	0	4	0.6	20	..	20	0.04	2.0	0
plus peanut butter	1 tablespoon	¾	21	**119**	5.5	9.7	3.4	14	0.5	160	..	6	0.09	4.2	0
plus salad	lettuce, beetroot, cucumber, tomato	1½	45	**12**	0.2	Tr	2.3	5	0.2	38	47	16	0.01	Tr	5
plus salmon	1 tablespoon	1	30	**49**	6.3	2.3	0	55	0.3	159	22	10	0.04	2.1	0
plus tomato	2 thin slices	½	13	**3**	Tr	Tr	0.5	2	0.1	1	16	8	Tr	0.1	3

MISCELLANEOUS—continued

Foods	Descriptive measure	Weight in ounces	Weight in grammes	Kilo-calories kcal	Protein g	Fat g	Carbo-hydrate g	Cal-cium mg	Iron mg	Sodium mg	Retinol activity µg	Thia-mine µg	Ribo-flavin mg	Niacin mg	Ascor-bic acid mg
Sauces and chutneys—															
Apple chutney	1 tablespoon	¾	21	43	0.2	Tr	11.0	6	0.2	36	..	..	..	..	..
Cheese sauce, medium	2 tablespoons	1⅝	47	84	3.7	6.1	3.6	103	0.1	257	48	14	0.10	Tr	Tr
Gravy, home made	2 tablespoons	1⅝	45	73	0.4	5.1	6.3	47	0.3	272	64	18	0.01	0.1	5
Tomato chutney	1 tablespoon	¾	21	32	0.2	Tr	13.0	6	0.2	27	..	..	..	..	..
Tomato ketchup and sauce	1 tablespoon	1¾	21	21	0.4	0.1	5.1	4	0.2	219	48	19	0.01	0.4	3
White sauce, medium savoury	2 tablespoons	1½	45	73	1.6	4.0	6.4	50	0.1	235	49	18	0.76	0.1	Tr
Soups, canned*—															
Chicken, cream of	1 cup	8	230	92	3.7	5.3	7.4	44	0.6	960	138	23	0.12	0.4	..
Split pea with ham	1 cup	8	230	177	8.7	3.7	27.4	23	3.3	363	32	138	0.09	1.1	..
Tomato, cream of	1 cup	8	230	87	1.3	2.3	15.3	30	0.7	960	65	46	0.07	0.5	..
Vegetable	1 cup	8	230	76	3.5	1.8	11.5	17	1.0	845	276	23	0.03	0.6	..
Soups, dried mix*															
Asparagus	1 cup	8	230	46	1.2	1.1	7.4	...	...	785	..	..	..	..	..
Chicken noodle	1 cup	8	230	31	1.7	0.6	7.3	...	...	710	..	..	..	..	..
Mushroom	1 cup	8	230	48	1.2	1.7	6.6	...	...	890	..	..	..	..	..
Tomato	1 cup	8	230	41	0.9	Tr	9.5	...	...	530	..	..	..	..	..
Spreads—															
Fish paste	1 teaspoon	..	5	7	0.9	0.2	0.3	23	0.3	74	..	..	..	..	..
Meat paste	1 teaspoon	..	5	10	0.7	0.7	0.2	1	0.2	40	..	..	..	..	..
Sugar, syrups, etc.—															
Honey	1 tablespoon	⅞	27	87	0.1	..	21.6	2	0.2	3	0	8	Tr	Tr	Tr
Jams and other preserves	1 tablespoon	⅞	27	71	Tr	Tr	17.9	5	0.2	3	0	1	Tr	Tr	1
Sugar, refined	1 tablespoon	⅝	16	62	0	0	16.0	Tr	Tr	Tr	0	0	0	0	0
brown	1 tablespoon	⅝	19	70	0	0	17.8	19	0.2	8	0	0	0	0	0

* Canned soups are prepared by diluting water (1:1) and Dried Mixes are prepared according to directions on the packet.